Shannonside Tales

By

John Casey

ISBN-13: 978-1-3999-9250-3
Front cover photography by Lee Williamson
Back cover photography by Joe McGrath
Book layout by Keith Millar
Jacket Concept by Andrew Knowles
Published by Rathcline Heritage Society, Lanesborough, Co. Longford

This book is dedicated to the people of
Ballyleague and Lanesborough
both living and who have passed into history.

CONTENTS

John Casey, Author, 2024.

INTRODUCTION

Some time last year (2023) I enjoyed the company of my friend John Casey, on a trip to the Guinness Storehouse in Dublin.

On this trip John regaled us with many stories, both humourous and otherwise, at one and the same time, had us in stitches or genuinely moved.

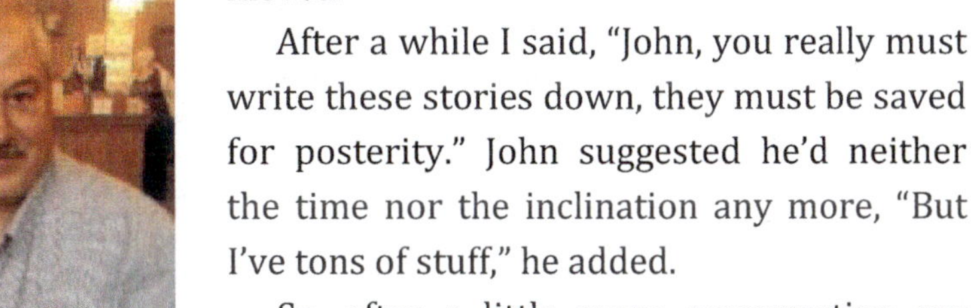

Andrew Knowles, Ballyleague, 2024

After a while I said, "John, you really must write these stories down, they must be saved for posterity." John suggested he'd neither the time nor the inclination any more, "But I've tons of stuff," he added.

So, after a little more conversation my spare room became the depository of many, many articles, books, letters, programmes, photographs, maps, magazines, John's own dissertation from Maynooth University, a book he had written for family only on his cousin, Fr. Joseph Murphy, and almost anything else he had been able to collect that was in anyway relative to Lanesborough/Ballyleague.

What follows is my attempt to cobble John's collections and writings into a coherent volume which we sincerely hope you will enjoy.

PREFACE

ACROSS THE DIVIDE

Lanesborough,
in the Parish of Rathcline,
County of Longford,
Diocese of Ardagh and Clonmacnois,
Province of Leinster.

Ballyleague,
in the Parish of Kilgefin,
County of Roscommon,
Diocese of Elphin,
Province of Connaught.

To understand the common link between the two communities divided by the majestic River Shannon it is necessary to examine the origins of the same communities. Béal Átha Liag or Ballyleague, the ancient name of Lanesborough says much about the origins of the town – translated the name means 'The mouth of the ford of the flagstones'. Before 1664 the town straddled both sides of the Shannon. George Lane was granted land on the Longford side of the river for services rendered to King Charles II and it was this monarch who gave a Royal Charter to George Lane. The town on the Longford side of the river dropped the name Béal Átha Liag or Ballyleague and became the Royal Borough of Lanesborough. The towns of Lanesborough and Ballyleague have indeed a long and distinguished history. This important crossing point on the Shannon has been a focus of life and activity for thousands of years.

Some family names are predominant and peculiar to this same area and give rise to evidence of a common linkage and interaction between people on both sides of the divide. Names such as Fallon, Hanley, etc, abound in the hinterland at the northern tip of Lough Ree. Thus, it was when the Great Famine struck like a massive hammer blow, the communities were once again united, though this time not in celebration like a wedding in days of old, but in misery and grief at the appalling havoc which decimated their parishes. The leading members of these same parishes made a joint appeal to the Crown authorities in Dublin Castle so as to make them aware of the magnitude of the plight facing the people who placed their trust in them.

Poised between two counties, two provinces and in olden times two Kingdoms, our community has received and assimilated influences from all over Ireland, and even further afield. Because of its location on the Shannon, our parishes are a mecca for visitors and fishermen from all over Europe.

Multi-cultureism is nothing new to our area, from the great influx of workers who became the backbone of the community when the bogs were opened up, to local individuals like Fr. Joseph Mullooly who hailed from Lehery, Lanesborough, and in the 1860s discovered the Miterium Temple under the Basilica of St. Clemente in Rome. There is even a Prince! from the Royal Family of Spain buried in the Abbey graveyard in Cloontuskert.

John Casey has spent a lifetime being enthralled by the history, events and people of this community. He has collected articles, letters, interviews and many many photographs of our place in the history of this land. What follows is a collection of these people, happenings and incidents which have made our community what it is today.

The writings are not entirely John's own. Much credit is due to two other local historians.

Firstly, Seán Ó Súilleabháin, from whose superb book, *LONGFORD'S REPUBLICAN STORY 1900 –2000*, much of the Lanesborough references in the chapter *TROUBLED TIMES* is taken. *(This book is a treasure-house and I would recommend it to anybody interested in our history — JC).*

Secondly, Tommy Murray, who writes with great feeling about his father Jim Murray in the chapter, "Memories of my Father's Forge". Tommy also contributed to the piece on the Mills and to the section on *THE SINN FÉIN WOMAN, CUMANN NA MBAN*, through his writings for the Longford Historical Society.

Tommy Murray

HISTORY
What is it?

It is often said that history is no more than the study of the human community. It details how people lived on a daily basis, shared ideas, how they rule or are ruled and how they fought. The word History derives from the Greek *'historia'*, information or an enquiry designed to elicit truth. The word story comes from the same source.

How did we get here?

This piece by Longford and Leitrim historian Seán Ó Súilleabháin explains the numerous ways that information can be gathered and how many of the chapters in this book were arrived at.

The most important sources for the study of practically every aspect of history of the past couple of hundred years are newspapers - local and national. The Irish nation and its people suffered grievously at the hands of British forces of occupation for many centuries but, here and there, someone in the British establishment made a decision that befitted all in the long run. This decision was the obligation placed on publishers of books and newspapers to deposit a copy of anything they published in the British Library in London and, in Ireland's case, in the National Library and Trinity College. *(The UK has four other copyright libraries: the Bodleian Library Oxford, Cambridge University Library, the National Library of Scotland and the National Library of Wales.)*

As wonderful an asset as this was, until the 1980s one had to travel to Dublin to access these records. Then came the facility to micro-film newspapers and the Longford County Library acquired microfilm of the *Longford Leader* and other local papers. Going to Dublin was no longer necessary. *Longford Leader* was first published in 1897. The icing on the cake came with digitalisation and you can now subscribe to ***www.Irishnewsarchive.com*** and view a wide range of papers from all over Ireland. With digitalisation came the 'search' facility which makes life even easier when searching for specific details or events.

Within the broad field of local history, genealogy or family history is one of the most interesting pursuits. As with newspapers, access to much of this information required trips to Dublin. Now, access to early censuses, birth, marriage and death records can be accessed at home online. The most important sources for family history are the church registers of baptism, marriage and death, and these can now be found online at ***www.rootsireland.ie***

Finally, there will be a section in each County Library that will contain books, photographs, maps even recordings relative to our local history. *(Much of John Casey's collection can be studied in the local Lanesborough Library.)*

Depending on the depth of research to be engaged in, one may still have to visit different libraries and archives, as well as interview people, but core research is certainly much quicker and easier than it used to be.

THE FIGHT FOR INDEPENDENCE

CHAPTER

1

TROUBLED TIMES

There were quite a number of events and participating locals from the Lanesborough area during the fight for independence, a few of which are detailed here:

Ambush at Scramogue – 23/03/21

The Strokestown–Longford road, (now the N5) was a busy road even in 1921. Almost every day British military lorries used it – it being a major communication route. So, while it might be considered ideal in respect of IRA ambushes, the frequency and volume of traffic made any such undertaking have to proceed with great caution. Men in an ambush position might be faced with two lorries when one was expected, or an escort of an armoured Lancia might bring up the rear. Sometimes there might be military traffic coming from both directions, as a consequence any planning by the IRA had to be elastic. There might have been any number of planned attacks that came to nothing because the volume of military traffic was greater than expected.

Volunteers from the slopes of Slieve Bawn in South Roscommon and from the Strokestown battalion in North Roscommon had come under the command of Seán Connolly. He was the Brigade Vice-Commandant of Longford and had been sent by GHQ to organise South Roscommon and to put it on some kind of fighting basis. He made the area active by attacking patrols and by an attempt to use explosives on a local barracks. He had come to Ballagh, under Slieve Bawn, to discuss a possible attack in Lanesborough. While he was in the area he examined the possibility of holding an ambush on the road crossing the Bogland to the Shannon, but of all the places Seán Connolly reconnoitered, the Scramogue position on the Strokestown–Longford road seemed the surest place.

An armoured Lancia of the period.

Kilgefin and Curraghroe companies remembered Connolly's eagerness to increase activity in their county so as to help out other regions by making the British withdraw some of their troops and resources from areas in which the local IRA brigades were coming under increasing pressure. However, before the Scramogue ambush, Brigade Vice-Commandant Connolly was himself killed in an ambush by the RIC Auxiliary Division at Selton Hill in Co. Leitrim. Connolly was running a training camp at Selton Hill; it is said he was informed upon by a local doctor who was ex-British Army. Six IRA members were killed in the attack.

The North and South Roscommon IRA brigades who were to take part in the ambush were now under the command of Patrick Madden. The brigade totalled 39 volunteers but only 14 took part in the attack. Several of the men recruited had served in the Irish Guards during the first World War but had been persuaded by Madden to join the IRA on their return. The ambush position was carefully planned, a farmhouse and barn on a bend had been taken over and a trench dug behind a hedge. The IRA men endured a long and uncomfortable wait until eventually a military lorry (unusually travelling unescorted) came their way. The lorry carried a nine man British Army and RIC patrol. The IRA opened fire from very close range, killing the driver and halting the lorry in its tracks. Several of the soldiers and policeman were hit as they scrambled for cover. The lorry had a Hotchkiss machine gun bolted to it, but the gunner only got one volley off before being badly wounded. The commander of the patrol, Captain Roger Grenville Peek, was wounded while on the lorry; he tried to run for safety but was hit again some 400 yards away. The only other officer, a Lieutenant Tennant, was also killed by a shotgun blast. After the death of the two officers, the surviving British, several of whom were wounded, surrendered. In addition to both officers two others of the patrol were killed, an RASC driver and one RIC Constable. Two men in civilian clothes were also found in the lorry – these turned out to be Black and Tan recruits who had been arrested by the RIC officers – one now dead – who were being transported to Longford. The ambush party, after taking the British arms including the Hotchkiss gun, also took as prisoners the two Black and Tans, and after burning the lorry they made their escape over the hill of Slieve Bawn.

The IRA leaders, Pat Madden, Luke Duffy and Frank Simons, decided to kill the two prisoners, even though they had offered to show the IRA men how to use the Hotchkiss gun. The IRA men reasoned that if the prisoners were free to identify any of the attackers then the volunteers would be at risk of being executed if captured. The two men were taken to remote locations and shot over the next two days.

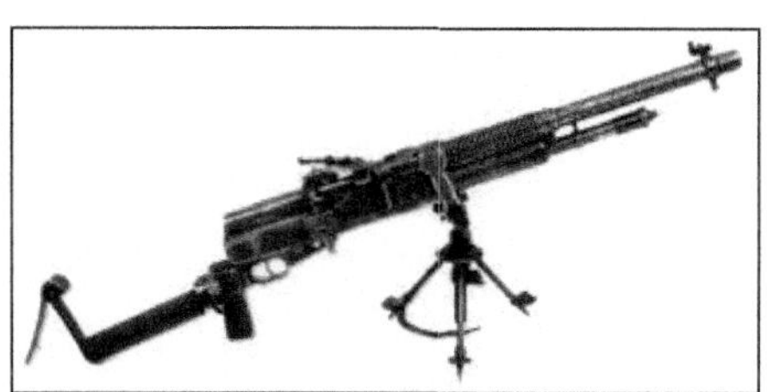

A Hotchkiss Gun.

The British garrison in Roscommon mounted a sweep of the area soon after the ambush. Eight lorries of soldiers and one whippet tank combed the area. Pat Mullooly and Brian Nagle were arrested and badly beaten by their captors on the road to Roscommon. Another, 'Cushy' Hughes, was picked up as he was drawing his soldiers pension in Roscommon. The next day, another volunteer, Michael Mullooly, was shot dead in his home by officers of the RIC.

The Longford Senior GAA Football Trophy – the Seán Connolly Cup.

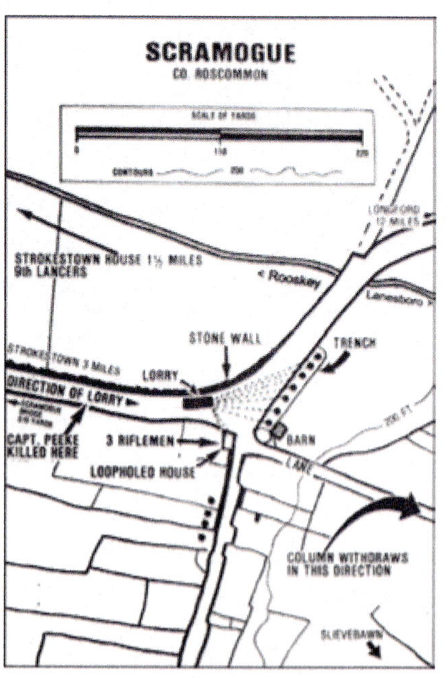

Patrick Belton

Possibly the most prominent figure from this area at the time would be Rathcline man, Patrick Belton. Born in 1884, Patrick Belton was clearly a scholarly man and after attending the local National School won a scholarship to Kings College London. He secured a position with the British Civil Service in London and at about the same time made the acquaintance of Michael Collins. He was present at the foundation of Sinn Féin in London and some sources suggest it was Patrick that initiated Michael Collins into the Irish Republican Brotherhood. He was also a prominent supporter of *Conradh na Gaeilge* or the Gaelic League which actively

MR. PATRICK BELTON,
Belfield Park, Drumcondra.

promoted the Irish language. He was a prominent member of the Geraldines GAA club in London and was for many years its president. In 1909 he became secretary of the London County Board of the GAA, though this was only a short lived position as in 1910 he was transferred to the Irish Land Commission in Dublin. During the rising, Belton was involved with the transfer of information and intelligence regarding the movement of arms.

After the rising he was suspended from the Land Commission after being suspected of involvement in it, but, one assumes due to lack of evidence against him he was re-instated. On 30/07/1918, Belton was arrested following a raid on his house where a quantity of arms and ammunition were discovered. The following month he was sentenced to six months imprisonment with hard labour. He served his sentence in Mountjoy and Belfast prisons. Belton was politically active his entire life, serving in Dáil Éireann for both Fine Gael and Fianna Fáil parties.

Patrick Belton was also founder and President of the Irish Christian Front. This was founded with the intention of showing support and raising funds for General Franco's Nationalist party in Spain. Patrick Belton died at his home in Killiney, South Dublin in January 1945.

The South Longford By-Election – 1917

The 1917 South Longford by-election resulted in a surprise victory for Sinn Féin and its candidate Joe McGuinness. This was a doubly surprising success. Firstly, the seat from 1882–1917 (six elections) had remained Unionist, all six elections being unopposed. Secondly, at the time of his victory, Joe McGuinness was languishing in an English jail, Lewes in East Sussex, for his part in the uprising. A native of Cloonmore townland, Tarmonbarry, Joe had taken part in the fighting at Four Courts. Following capture he

Joe McGuinness.

was sentenced to ten years penal servitude, later reduced to three.

That Sinn Féin won this election was in no doubt, helped by the canvassing of some of the biggest hitters in the movement. Michael Collins and Arthur Griffith, family members of those executed in 1916 such as Margaret Pearse - mother of Padraig, Tom Clarke's widow Kathleen and Count and Countess Plunkett – parents of Joseph Mary Plunkett, all came to the area to speak on behalf of Joe. Also a number of the younger Catholic priests, such as Fr. Edward Ryans of Lanesborough gave voice in support of the Sinn Féin candidate. That said, not all the clergy were supportive. Fr. Peter O'Connor of Newtown Forbes preached very anti-Sinn Féin sermons.

In the end it was a victory of very fine margins.

BY-ELECTION RESULT SOUTH LONGFORD 1917	
Joe McGuinness (Sinn Fein)	1498
Paddy McKenna (Irish Parliamentary Party)	1461

Assaults on Barracks

Prime targets for the IRA at this time were the various barracks spaced around the county. Barracks were full of guns and ammunition which was the main reason for attacking them. By 1920 such had been the effect of these countywide attacks that only six barracks remained open in the whole County Longford. These were the barracks in Longford town, Edgeworthstown, Granard, Ballymahon, Drumlish and Lanesborough. An order was issued to burn down all vacant barracks and this was complied with over the Easter weekend 1920. A major coup for the IRA in August of that year was the taking of the Ballymahon barracks.

This turned out to be a significant event for the IRA and a major embarrassment for the authorities. The attack was brilliantly planned by Seán MacEoin and Seán Connolly. Designed to take place at midnight, all roads bar one into Ballymahon were blocked. After the raid had taken place and an escape made down the one road still open, this road too was blocked by felled trees, making pursuit almost impossible.

The raid was affected by entering Donoghues Saddlers two doors down from the barracks. From here a hole was knocked through the wall giving access to the home of the Lloyd family who lived next to the barracks. Part of the ceiling was ripped down here giving access to the roof space above the barracks. While all this was happening inside, a party of IRA men were firing shots at the door and windows of the barracks by way of occupying those inside. At this point, a home-made bomb of sulphur, black pepper, brimstone and other ingredients was dropped down into the barracks. Gas fumes filled the rooms, resulting in the surrender of the RIC men inside.

This was in fact the first time for MacEoin and Connolly that RIC men had surrendered to the IRA, and not one casualty was incurred by either side. A good quantity of arms and ammunition were captured and taken from the barracks. One of the men involved in this raid was Michael Joseph Ryan, a Lanesborough man, who owned the lorry that carried the bombs and IRA weapons to Ballymahon.

Michael Joseph Ryan

Michael Joseph Ryan was a cousin of, and lived with, Dr. Joseph O'Halloran, the doctor who is the subject of another chapter in this book. From 1917–'20 he was a major figure in the republican movement in the Lanesborough area. Michael Ryan owned a garage in the town and crucially a car as well. In 1917 he returned home to Co. Clare to support Sinn Féin in the by-election there and ended up transporting Eamon De Valera around the constituency. In 1918 a dispute between Michael Ryan and the Captain of the Lanesborough company, over the recruiting to the company of two protestant men, came to blows in Tullyvrane school. This was a significant enough event to result in Michael Collins coming to the area and presiding over a Court Martial, the outcome of which was demotion for both men.

In 1919 prominent republican Ernie O'Malley was badly injured in a shoot out near Ballymoe in Co. Roscommon. Michael Ryan, being in possession of a car was called on to transport the injured O'Malley to Dublin. En route, somewhere near Mullingar, they encountered an RIC foot patrol, Ryan drove through the patrol while the injured O'Malley managed to throw a grenade through the window at the RIC men, despite being fired on by the patrol they made it through unscathed.

Michael Ryan was less fortunate in Carrickedmond in late 1920. An explosion occurred which severely injured Ryan in the hip. Not wishing to worry his wife he decided to return home, however he was barely through the door when the house was surrounded by RIC officers and he was arrested. He ended up in the Ballykinlar Internment Camp on the Co. Down coast in Northern Ireland where he was held until Christmas 1921.

Ballykinlar Internment Camp.

Shot dead in Fallons

This is one of the most complex stories of any that came out of the struggle for Independence in this area. A number of different versions have been recorded for one reason or another but, as best we can make out, what follows is 'probably' what happened.

In April 1921, it is thought while playing cards, Constable Albert William Smith, a 36 year old Englishman was shot dead in Fallons Tailors shop (now Joe O'Briens) in Lanesborough. John O'Sullivan, an apprentice tailor, was one of the card players and was also a member of the IRA.

What happened next has been disputed over the years, but the story goes that Constable Smith's new revolver was on the table and he showed John O'Sullivan how to use it. While handling the gun himself, John O'Sullivan possibly dropped it on the floor whereby it discharged itself causing Constable Smith to be hit and dying of the injury. O'Sullivan was arrested and brought before a court of enquiry but wasn't charged with any offence.

District Inspector Gleeson who was in charge in Lanesborough, and thought to favour the republican cause, ensured that the matter went no further. The *Longford Leader* reported that the revolver "fell out of Constable Smith's holster, went off, fatally wounding him in the mouth". In later years, possibly thinking of war pensions that were available, a number of men claimed to be in on the 'ambush' of Constable Smith but nothing was ever proved.

The Turlough Ambush

The area known as The Turlough (where in the late 1800s horse races were held) is in the townland of Cashel Beg. On 17th May 1921 a bicycle patrol of 'Tans' was coming from Lanesborough, heading for Newtowncashel when they were ambushed by members of the South Longford Flying Column under O/C Bernard Garrahan.

Constable Kenyon and another Tan had gone into Hanley's house to return fire on the volunteers, whilst opening a window Constable Kenyon was shot through the eye. Two other RIC men were wounded in the attack. The Hanley family members at home took shelter in other rooms, terrified while the ambush was in progress.

Locals, it was reported, claimed that the company of RIC and Tans scattered in all directions, discarding as they went their outer clothes so that their grey undergarments enabled them to blend in with the grey stone walls, which they crept along behind making their way back to Lanesborough and safety.

One of the discarded jackets was found in the garden of Pat Farrell of Lismacmanus; inside the jacket was found a Policeman's Whistle, and a letter which read as follows:

My dear Wife,
I am sending you £5 to put new Linoleum on the back kitchen. I hope the baby is keeping well and I will see you soon if I survive this conflict.
Your loving husband.

The *Longford Leader* reported:
The remains of police constable Kenyon who was shot in the Turlough Ambush on Tuesday last evening were conveyed to England for internment and were awarded a military funeral. The remains were carried to the station on a military wagon covered with a Union Jack

and preceded by a detachment of the 9th Lancers, Auxiliary RIC, and the officers in charge. The band of the 9th Lancers played Chopin's funeral march and a number of ex- servicemen also took part in the procession.

Back in Lanesborough, the auxiliaries in a rage of revenge at the death of one of their comrades, ordered twelve of the most prominent men on the Main Street to line up against the barracks wall and were proposing to shoot them – though there was doubt they would carry out the threat.

However, before any such action could be taken, Head Constable Gleeson walked between the auxiliaries and the 'Condemned Men', saying: "You will have to shoot me first", he then ordered the auxiliaries out of Lanesborough, but they didn't leave before, in anger, shooting the chimney pots off the barracks roof.

Shortly afterwards, Head Constable Gleeson resigned from the RIC in protest at the behaviour of the Crown forces in Ireland.

THE SINN FÉIN WOMAN

Tommy Murray, who has contributed much, both to this book and to local history in general, had a more personal tale to tell when in 2019 he wrote a piece for the Journal of the County Longford Historical Society on his maternal grandmother, Bridget Farrell of Lisnacrusha, Lanesborough.

The following are excerpts taken directly from that article.

Born in 1883, Bridget married Ned Farrell in October 1905, settling in the Stretford area of Manchester, England. Two years later in 1907 Mary, their first daughter arrived, they were to go on and have a family of twelve, eight of whom survived.

Bridget's already keen political awareness was strengthened, whilst working as a nurse, by the discrimination and racism she saw levelled against the Irish community. She came from a family of strong Republican beliefs, had ancestors slain at the battle of Ballinamuck and longed to see Ireland free from the yoke of British sovereignty.

In Britain, after the 1916 uprising had been suppressed, thousands of young Irish men and a considerable number of Irish women were rounded up, transported and interred in various English jails often in very primitive conditions. At this point Bridget got involved (this from her testimony to the Irish Pensions Board) and began by organising groups of Irish girls to do church gate collections so that food parcels and essentials could be brought to the prisoners in the different jails.

This was just a start to Bridget's activism. She organised placard carrying groups of girls to march, demanding that the prisoners be given political status. These girls suffered much abuse:

'We got mud dashed in our faces and rotten oranges thrown at us, but we kept on.... (I arranged for) groups of good singers to sing outside the prisons' gates every night. (They sang songs) such as Fontenay, father Murphy, Davitt's Lament and the soldier's song. We were pushed off. Still we cried out, 'give our Irish soldiers political treatment'. 'The English women drowned us with water...'

Bridget gave an account of another form of activism, this time against a British politician, Sir Hamar Greenwood.

Greenwood, who in later years would become Chief Secretary, had a large investment in the Wigan Coalfield, and sold most of his coal in Manchester.

'So I immediately set out and got my Tipperary girls... to go from door to door carrying placards and asking that they get no coal from Greenwood. We did splendid at this; the Irish women hunted Greenwood's coalmen...'

This tactic must have put pressure on Greenwood who, in turn, most likely put pressure on other politicians to have the matter resolved. In any case, many of the Irish prisoners languishing in English jails were released in the final months of 1916.'

Early in 1917 Bridget's husband Ned was called back to Lisnacrusha to take over the family farm. So, back in Ireland at a critical time in the struggle for independence, Bridget threw herself wholeheartedly into whatever she could do locally.

The South Longford By-Election 1917

A by-election had been called for South Longford and Joe McGuinness from Cloonmore, Tarmonbarry was the candidate. (See chapter Troubled Times – **The South Longford By - Election 1917)**. Bridget threw herself into the campaign to get McGuinness elected.

In her own words, she states:

I drilled 200 children and marched them through the streets of Lanesborough, Strokestown, Dromod and Longford town, fed them with sandwiches at my own expense for the Joe McGuinness election campaign. I dressed five young children in the tri-colours, and each held a key.... at the door of each polling station, each child pleading and presenting the key to any and everyone that (was) against our cause. 'Take the key and let out the prisoners free, and vote for Joe McGuinness', and, at intervals, marched the town singing all sorts of republican songs'.

Why Strokestown? It can only be assumed that she similarly supported the election of Count Plunkett in North Roscommon in February of the same year.

Bridget was elected first President of the newly formed Rathcline branch of the Cumann na mBan at a meeting held in Tullyvrane School, at a meeting that was attended by, amongst others, Miss Alice Cooney, later to become the wife of General Seán MacEoin. Bridget recalled that one of her first duties as President was to set up First Aid classes with a view to providing members with the skills to dress the wounds of the volunteers in the struggle that was surely to come.

Bridget Farrell.

Other activities included fund-raising for the families of republican prisoners and other nationalist causes. Weekly drill classes were also held.

Darrel Figgis, the Irish writer and Sinn Féin activist was sent to South Longford to help with the campaign to elect Joe McGuinness, in this capacity he came in contact with Bridget Farrell on a number of occasions. After McGuinness was elected, Figgis presented Bridget with a silver mounted umbrella, so impressed was he with her activities, he said to her: *'If we had ten women like you, we would have a free Ireland.'*

Another incident that Bridget was involved in took place in 1918, when, although the War of Independence wasn't in full swing, there were already skirmishes and confrontations with the Forces of the Crown.

At one such incident, Ernie O'Malley was wounded escaping from arrest by the RIC at Ballymoe. He made good his escape by swimming across the River Suck and being cared for in various safe-houses. Eventually he was hidden in McCrann's shed, right under the noses and over the road from the barracks in Lanesborough. He was secretly smuggled out and driven to Dublin via Mullingar.

This was only possible because of the treatment O'Malley had received from Bridget. In her 1951 submission she states:

> *'It was I and Mrs McCrann and Hannah Martin attended to Ernie O'Malley's wounds in McCrann's shed in the middle of the night. Only for I he would have bled to end his life.'*

The War of Independence 1919–21 saw no let up in the nationalist activities conducted by Bridget.

After Sinn Féin's sweeping victories in the 1918 elections, Dáil Éireann was set up and met for the first time in January 1919. Later that year Sinn Féin was outlawed and the conflict became more intense. The IRA used guerrilla tactics, burning RIC barracks, forcing others to be abandoned, capturing arms, organising ambushes and disrupting communications. Many RIC members were killed or injured and in the spring of 1920 the British in an attempt to quell the IRA, introduced support for the RIC, in the force that was known, with revulsion, as the Black and Tans. They were followed by the Auxiliaries. The Auxiliary Division of the RIC was a para-military police unit, which, with very few exceptions, accepted only ex-officers from the British Army (or one of the Empire armies). They served as separate units to the RIC who had very little control over them.

Bridget threw herself wholeheartedly into this phase of the struggle. In addition to her role as President of Cumann na mBan, she was providing a 'safe house' for local volunteers 'on the run'.

Bridget lost her 1951 application to be granted Pension rights and in her appeal to this decision stated:

> *'I washed, cooked, baked cakes, left open doors, all the tools at their use, anything they needed to dig the roads around here it was our tools that they used'.* She went on, *'Tom Robinson (IRA officer) took men here night after night, I fed them washed their shirts and on one occasion we had a pig in salt and it just lasted them a week,* (a pig would normally last a household half a year!) I *left my own children without milk many times, to leave it for them.'*

According to Michael Brennan, IRA Commandant County Clare, the 'Flying Columns' would have collapsed without Cumann na mBan, in dispatch carrying, finding and the providing of guns, scouting and intelligence work, all of which are highly dangerous, they did far more than the soldiers.

Bridget obviously held very staunch republican views and came from an ardently republican family, it is a little more than surprising then that her brother James McNally, Kilmore, was a member of the RIC. However, James must also have had republican sympathies, for when he realised the force was being used to subjugate the Irish people, he resigned.

In fact he became an intelligence officer and dispatch carrier for the IRA under the guise of an insurance salesman, cycling around the locality.

Bridget stated:

> *'He helped and succeeded in catching a spy for captain Kenny, who shot him. This spy did a terrible lot of harm getting fellows arrested... The Tans beat a couple of fellows they found through this spy.... .*
>
> *I was told by Dev (De Valera) that one RIC resignation was better than ten ambushes'...*

This statement seems to suggest that Bridget knew De Valera, or at least spoke to him personally.

Bridget was particularly fond of training young boys in drill and presenting arms, using wooden replicas or Hurley sticks. She had used this tactic at the aforementioned election campaigns.

She wrote:

'I drilled 200 children and, to defy the Tans' I marched them down the street of Lanesborough and halted them at the RIC barracks. Only for Inspector Gleeson the Tans would have shot Hanna Martin and myself. He came out and told me to disperse... we sang all the songs so hurtful to England...

To-day (1951) the biggest part of them boys are in America, and on St. Patrick's night in Longford hall, U.S.A., they gave a rousing cheer for Mrs. Farrell, Lisnacusha...

Sadly, as we know, the Civil War broke out following the signing of the Anglo-Irish treaty. It was waged between June 1922 and May 1923 between the forces of the new Free State and the republican opposition forces who did not accept the Treaty.

In her 1951 submission she wrote:

'Now came the worst time of all. I stuck with Dev, through thick and thin. My parish priest turned on me on polling day (Irish Pact General Election 1922) *when I tried to convince people to vote for Dev's crowd. I once held a meeting under the veil of a farmers Wives Association to get all their votes for Dev, and again, thank God, succeeded, when no one wanted the 'irregulars'.'*

It must have been a traumatic moment for Bridget when her parish priest turned on her as she was a devout Catholic, she didn't waver but continued to support the Republican side in a tangible way, she wrote:

'I left the door open for the boys 'on the run' and told them to keep their courage (which) was needed more then than with (against) the Tans', as the boys (the treaty forces) knew all the haunts. And it was sadder in Roscommon (where) I was known as the 'Republican Woman'.'

In this article Tommy Murray asks the question:

> *'Do you think this woman deserved a certificate under the military service pensions Act?'*

Her submission was refused, she appealed to the Board of Assessors in 1942 with further appeals coming in 1945 and 1951:

> *'Oscar Traynor* (Minister of Defence at the time of her first application) *insulted me terrible by telling me, 'you are not the person to whom the Act applies'.'*

So, here was a woman who was honoured by Darrell Figgis, saved Ernie O'Malley's life, was a collaborator of Joe McGuinness, was well known by Seán MacEoin and appears to have been on speaking terms with De Valera, yet was denied the recognition she deserved, in her old age.

In her 1942 appeal to the Board of Assessors she asks:

> *'I want to know the meaning of this? General Seán MacEoin told me that he got a letter from the Pension Board with my name in the approved group, and passed by the Board. There is something wrong. Who verified me? Who got my name taken off the list?.... we want to show our people how we were wronged. there is a man here (local) that is allowed to verify for people that is not and never was a sworn IRA during his life. I will have this brought up in the Dáil!'*

This indignation is suggestive that something underhand had occurred in relation to her application, and may refer to the fact that her family had uncovered information that a certain individual from the locality who was either a referee or had the ear of a referee, had spoken against her and had her application turned down, because, she had information which, if made known, would seriously jeopardise his own status as a man to whom the Act did apply.

Although never given, by the state, the recognition Bridget deserved, this omission was somewhat assuaged on her death.

From the LONGFORD LEADER, January 1956

The death of Mrs Bridget O'Farrell took place at her husband's residence in Lisnacusha on Thursday 29th December 1955, after a brief illness. Deceased passed peacefully away surrounded by members of her family and fortified by the rites of the Church. The remains were removed to St. Mary's Church, Lanesborough, and a large gathering of friends, including General Seán Mac Eoin, Minister of Defence, attended the removal.

The funeral on Saturday was one of the largest seen in the village in recent years. A Guard of Honour made up of old IRA comrades was drawn up outside the Church, and the coffin, draped in the Tri-Colour, was carried and escorted to the outskirts of Lanesborough. The cortege, a mile long, wended its way to Rathcline graveyard where the last post was sounded. Rev Fr. O'Grady officiated at the graveside. R.I.P.

She was mourned by her husband Edward O'Farrell, Patrick, Edward and Joseph (sons), Mrs. Mary Murray, Mrs. Annie Glennon, Mrs. Hannah Fayne, Mrs. Bridget Connaughton and Mrs Philomena Gallagher (daughters).

She was the first President of Cumann na mBan and it was one of the first branches to organise Red Cross classes and lectures. Her most treasured possession was the silver-mounted umbrella presented to her by the late Darrell Figgis.

For herself, she was kind, generous, charitable, a staunch friend and a mother always exact in the duties of her station.

Let the words she often quoted be her epitaph:

Kindness in another's troubles, courage in your own.

Ar dheis Dé go raibh a h-anam.

Rev. Dr. Thomas Hurley

Canon Hurley was a native of Ballymoe, just over the Roscommon border in County Galway. He served as the parish priest in Ballagh from 1918–'46. Father Hurley was a friend of 'the boys'. One Sunday morning as he was conducting Mass, he looked up and saw a group of Black and Tans coming in the main door of Ballagh Church. Father Hurley knew that many of the parishioners were Volunteers, and would be armed. During those years, to have been caught and arrested carrying a gun was a sure ticket to one of any number of 'His Majesty's Inns'. Quick thinking saved the day.

Father Hurley called for the two oldest men in the parish, and his own young servers, to carry the processional cross and candles down the main aisle. He then went to confer with the leader of the military. Assured that no harm would come to the general population, he returned to the altar and completed Mass. He did announce that the policemen were looking for specific men, who would no doubt be armed. At the conclusion of the final 'Amen', priest and flock reverently walked down the aisle and gathered outside beyond the entrance.

The Volunteers within had sufficient opportunity to drop their guns and ammunition belts on the floor inside the Church, before following the congregation outside. The local girls, ever the tough and ready supporters, hid the weapons inside the confessional.

Even during the day-to-day battles with the British Force, Canon Hurley was ever available to the Volunteers in matters of both material and spiritual natures.

* "It was quite a usual thing to find him pacing up and down the road outside the house we were holding a meeting or having a meal."

God bless Father Hurley! He died in 1955.

* *Frank Simons Volunteer Witness statement to the Bureau of military history 1913–'21.*

Help from the Islands *Tommy Murray*

The islands of Lough Ree and their inhabitants were not untouched by the hostilities of the War of Independence. The people of Inchenagh Island played no small part in the struggle by providing a place of refuge and succour for the Volunteers from both sides of the lake. My father Jim and his brother Tom were both members of the Kilteevan Company, 3rd Battalion of the Volunteers in Co. Roscommon. Both of them took refuge with their mothers' people on the island when things got too hot on the mainland. My father did tell me however that they had an excellent hideout/dugout in Clooncraff Bog, whenever the Tans raided the village.

By April 1919, Co. Roscommon was declared a "disturbed area" by the British authorities and a reign of terror began. As the struggle progressed the 3rd Battalion and its constituent companies was active:

drilling, raiding for firearms, carrying out ambushes and disrupting transport and communications. Shootings, arrests, beatings, interrogations and other acts of terror were carried out by the military, mostly by the Tans and Auxiliaries stationed in Roscommon town. By this time many outlying barracks such as Athleague, Fourmilehouse and Beechwood were closed down and their forces withdrawn to Roscommon.

One of the main tactics of the Volunteers was to make travel, transport and communications difficult for the forces of the Crown. In the spring of 1921, the Cloontuskert Company of Volunteers opened a trench on the Roscommon–Lanesborough road at Cloontymullen. The Tans and Auxiliaries from the barracks in Roscommon filled it in again but, secretly placed a landmine in it. It lay untouched for a while but, some time later John Scally of Gallagh and some of his comrades including his namesake John Scally of Portnahinch; Johny Connor, Lisinaria; Peter Egan, Portnahinch; Johny Kelly, Antrabeg and Jimmy Gannon, Weekfield, all from the Cloontuskert Company, had set about the task of reopening the trench when an explosion occurred, injuring four of them. My father and others from the Kilteevan Company were on the hill of Ballinaboy, acting as scouts on the lookout for British Forces, when they heard the explosion.

The injured were first taken to Portnahinch where their wounds were dressed, and from there by boat to Inchenagh island as a safe haven from the British Forces. Mention should be made here of the many female volunteers who helped with the dressing of wounds and the hiding of Volunteers, when necessary.

Of the four injured men, John Kelly and John Connor were the most severely wounded. The former was subsequently taken to a Dublin hospital where he had a plate inserted in his stomach. John Connor had shrapnel in his hip and a piece of his ear blown off. Perhaps the most unlucky of all was John Scally who had some injuries to his legs but was not considered in any danger until that is, he developed lead poisoning. The lead eyelets of his boots had penetrated his flesh with the force of the explosion. Alas, despite the best efforts of his carers, he died on 11th May 1921.

My father and other Volunteers from Kilteevan, under the command of Matt Davis, were involved in the secret removal of his body from the island to Kilteevan Cemetery, where he was buried at night by his comrades from the local companies of Volunteers. Great care was taken to leave no trace of a burial, as the Crown Forces were still searching the graveyards of the region in the sure understanding that some of the men involved in the reopening of the trench must have been severely or mortally wounded at the scene. The Tans searched Kilteevan graveyard thoroughly a few days later but could find no trace of the newly-made grave.

Some time after the Truce, John Scally's body was exhumed and re-interred with full military honours and in the presence of all his comrades, in Cloontuskert Cemetery. My father, who was in the guard of honour, told me it was a very warm summers day and having stood for three hours in Kilteevan Cemetery, the members of the guard walked beside the cortege all the way to Cloontuskert Cemetery, and there stood to attention for another hour, for the re-internment.

Who were the Black and Tans?

As we have just read, in the spring of 1921, the Black and Tans were active in Co. Roscommon. Recruited from among the thousands of ex-NCOs who had seen service in the Great War of 1914–'18, they received cursory training in police work before being turned loose on the Irish.

In Ireland, they were expected to act as a prop to the Royal Irish Constabulary, among whom resignations, general low morale and a flow of recruits thinning to a trickle had seriously impaired functional efficiency. The paucity of correctly fitting police uniforms created a situation where instead of parading in regulation Constabulary outfit, the ex-NCOs were rigged out in a confused array of British Army Khaki and RIC dark bottle-green. This blend of the two uniforms inspired some wit to name them Black and Tans after the famous pack of Limerick Foxhounds ...

The British government equipped them with rifles and revolvers and bountiful ammunition, paid them ten-shillings a day and ranked them as police constables. Their conduct in Ireland was such that Winston Churchill himself complained that where the Tans were concerned, 'casual looting and thieving, as well as drunkenness and gross disorder are occurring'. Even the men of the RIC found their new British allies socially undesirable.

The Auxiliaries were a tough unsympathetic bunch of British ex-Officer Adventurers, Royal Engineers among them. Braver and brainier than the ruffianly Black and Tans but just as ruthless.

The 'Auxies' as they became known, were like the Tans recruited to help the dwindling RIC. They were intended to deal out rough justice to the Irish insurgents. The 'Auxies' were ranked as police sergeants and paid a pound a day. They were identifiable by their Glengarry bonnets set to one side.

SOME NOTABLE REIDENTS

CHAPTER

2

LANESBOROUGH MEMORIES

John Casey, our renowned local historian, has collected over many years, stories, tales and the folklore of Lanesborough and the surrounding areas. He recalls the characters of his youth, his schooldays, early work and all other matters that were interesting to an inquisitive mind.

Some time ago now, he jotted down the very earliest of his memories and recollections (you will be amazed at just how early), and committed them to paper. This is what he wrote. *(Ed.)*

The year was 1938 and the Great Creator decided it was my time to visit Mother Earth. St. Peter called me into his office that was situated near the front gate, and thus instructed the Archangel Michael to draw up the contract. Michael was in charge of all the dispatches down to earth, I duly signed the contract. I was then given my instructions as to what I could and could NOT do on Earth. Peter informed me I could have until the 2038, he added that most people are back long before this length of time but I'd been granted a longer stay than most. Peter then instructed Michael to bring me to the boss to get my final blessing. As I knelt before that most holy of faces I could not but notice the tears that were streaming down his cheeks and running into his lovely white beard. So, I asked Peter what was the matter with him? "Ah, it's that blackguard Hitler that is causing him to be so sad!"

I was then taken outside of the gates, I'd never been outside before and it all looked very strange and exciting at the same time. I was instructed to make my way to a stable where an angel would be waiting, with a stork. I was told to sit in the special seat designed to bring me safely down the earth. I'd just got in, put my seat-belt on and was ready for takeoff when a breathless St. Peter rushed out of his office and engaged with the angel.

I was ordered out and the angel returned the stork to the stable. He soon returned with a stork twice the size of the first and this one had two seats on its back, with the word twins written on the side. At this point, a small door to the side of the big gate opened and a small girl walked out and sat on the seat next to me. Everything now seemed in order for our journey to begin. I asked the stork if he knew the way and did he know the family we were going to. He said not to worry, he did know the family, and that he had even delivered twins there before, but sadly he said he thought one of them had been sent back...

***

My earliest real memories would be from the middle of the wartime. At the age of about 4 or 5, say 1942–'44. At this time my father had a Baby Ford motor car that he had purchased before the war. I can clearly recall being taken for a ride through the parish. He stopped outside one particular house and began talking to a man – Tom Hunt was his name – and I can remember him wearing a hard hat, but I don't recall why. I also remember he gave me some cartridges, used of course, but I was thrilled to have them.

I don't think we were able to afford the car after the war so my dad sold it to a man from Fourmilehouse for £5. This man had the vehicle converted to a pick-up truck for collecting eggs, and you could see it passing through Lanesborough every week on its way to Dublin.

***

It was in the summer of 1944 that the second World War became all too real for young and old alike in our part of Ireland.

At that time an American plane crashed between Strokestown and Roscommon. When it had been collected they had to bring it through Lanesborough but when they got to the bridge, the wings were too wide to enable it to cross, so they had to be removed. Can you just imagine the excitement.

I didn't know much about the war at all then but I do remember looking inside one of the windows on the plane and being very disappointed that there were no Germans with guns inside. It was an American plane after all, but the imagination runs wild.

A 1937 Baby Ford similar to the one John's father owned.

I recall being told and shown that the Irish Army had put tar barrels and large stones in the middle of fields that could conceivably be used to land a German plane on. The Square Park on the Longford road had them.

(At the time there was utmost secrecy about the event – it wasn't reported in the papers or the radio. After the war it was disclosed that the plane was actually a Canadian bomber and some malfunction in its system had led to a fuel leak. the pilot managed to down the plane in a field and despite considerable damage to the aircraft's body, all four occupants walked away from the scene.)

***

A Red Kerry cow, similar to the one our family had.

At this time, as a family we had an ass and cart and also a cow but, at that time we had no land. In those times almost every house in town would own a cow. We were no different and we would regularly make our own butter. When the churn was filled and ready to start the churning process my mother would dust a little salt on the outside, This, she said would banish away all the evil spirits, also, if the butter was slow in coming she would sprinkle onto the churn just a little holy water and that would do the trick in no time.

***

One August summers day, the Gallagher brothers, my three brothers and myself, travelled to the sports day in Killashee, in our ass and cart. When we arrived at Hands Hill, just the Lanesborough side of Killashee, the ass went on strike! It stopped, lay down under the cart and refused to budge. It was a warm day, so we removed his tack and proceeded to pull the cart up the hill ourselves. On seeing this, the ass happily trotted along beside us.

Eventually we managed to find the field where the sports were to be held, just outside that magnificent city of Killashee! My brother Michael won the first race and Eddie Casey of Killashee was second. However, Eddie had a brother on the committee and it was decided that Eddie had romped home in first place. Such a row broke out between the two Casey clans over this act of poor sportsmanship that our little party ended up making a hasty retreat from the field, and left in such a hurry that we went without the ass and cart and the medals we had won.

We had to call on a neutral party to venture to Killashee and retrieve our ass and cart and medals the next day.

***

Just down the Strokestown Road lived our postman and we would look forward to greeting him every morning we could. This was not to collect letters you understand, but for the wondrous stories he would tell us.

He would regale us with tales about the rabbits and the birds he met and spoke with as he was doing his rounds. He would explain how many children Mrs Rabbit had, what the birds got up to first thing in the morning, any number of tales he would happily tell.

***

A vivid memory from this time is the occasion of a visit from America of a cousin who was a priest. Such family members were held in the highest of regard, and to us it was like the President himself was coming to tea. We'd had a new path laid from front door to street, the front of the shop had been painted and new curtains put up in all the windows.

The four of us were out in the fields but we were told in no uncertain terms to be back in the house by 3 o'clock sharp so that we would be all nice and shiny for the newly ordained family priest. The priest was to be collected off the train by the local taxi from Longford station. Anyway, we were not in by 3 o'clock! It was probably nearer 4 o'clock when we started back up the road to Lanesborough. We hadn't gone very far when who should pull up beside us but the taxi carrying our priest. The taxi driver told Father Joe who we were and he invited us into the car, even though we had no shoes, mucky faces and scattered hair.

Our mother, father, sisters and a whole host of relations were gathered on the street waiting for the grand arrival. You should have seen my mother's face when the car stopped and who should jump out first, but four scruffy urchins!

Schooldays

Our teachers were the Master and Mistress. Mr. and Mrs. Edward Rhattigan. Master Ned we knew him as.

I can recall very little of the education I got! But what I can recall most vividly is the arrival every year of Duffy's Circus. The colourful circus tent was put up in Big Paddy's field, just in front of the school. We were always delighted to see the Master go out and shake hands with John Duffy for this made the circus respectable. John Duffy was an old man then and I remember him sitting on a chair watching on keenly as the big top was erected. I loved the circus, the distinct smell of the exotic animals and the trampled grass. My father loved it as well and I think he was just as excited as I was.

A big event would be the day the school inspector turned up. On this day the Master would send someone into town to buy a sweet cake. He would only have one slice himself, and at the end of the day put what was left into the press or cupboard. Joe and I observed this, so later that evening we made our way back to school and got in via the back door, it was easy if you knew how. Anyway, we decided to have just one slice each, but inevitably, one led to two and then three, and then the cake was gone.

The next day when the Master opened the press at lunchtime he was somewhat at a loss, he just scratched his head and closed it again. I guess he thought the Mistress had taken it home. Another little trick Joe and I played was a bit more naughty. On our way to school one morning we noticed that Harold's (a general purpose shop situated on the main road just above where Adie's bar is now) had a new line in sweets. Of course, we had no money ... how to get some? We thought of a plan.

On the way into school, having checked no one was watching, we let the air out of one of the tyres on the Master's bike. We went in and told him it was punctured. "Oh good children, good children, will you take it down to Harold's and get it fixed." With that he put his hand in his pocket and brought out a shiny new half-crown. So, we went down to Harold's, got a loan of his pump and pumped it back up. We told the Master the puncture had cost one shilling and gave him back 1/6d in change.

The Master said we were very good boys ... and we had a shilling to spend on Harold's new range of sweets.

***

The couple in the centre of the picture are the Master and Mistress on their honeymoon in Kerry in 1911. They went on to have eight daughters and one son.

First Holy Communion is always a big event. The priest had informed us that we would have to go to confession to tell of our sins. Of course at that age (and ignoring what's written above) I had no sins, so unblemished in character was I, that I was going to have to create one!

One morning on my walk to school I thought of a good sin. Liza Clyne had a white door so I decided to give it a good kick and run. I was now satisfied, I had a good sin for the priest.

***

Our cow was a small Red Kerry, though to the townsfolk she was known as Mick Casey's cow. She was kept in a smallish triangular field on the outskirts of town. In her blood must have been how her ancestors roamed the beautiful hills of Kerry, for she really didn't like being confined to such a small field. In fact, more often than not she could be found wandering on the road, or worse, in some neighbour's garden.

About this time the new Bord na Móna houses were being constructed, and she loved the new grass, much to the annoyance of the caretaker. This caretaker would drive her down through the town as far as our house and call out my father, he'd then say if my father didn't keep the cow under control he'd shoot the thing.

This didn't bother my father too much because he said she always had very rich milk after feasting on Bord na Móna grass. She also had a penchant for the grass around the church, and on one occasion went in through the porch and drank the holy water out of the font!

When it was time for her to go and see the bull, she would find her way up to Sonny Rhattigans by herself! Sonny would open the gate and let her in to see the bull. When all the necessaries had been completed Sonny would open the gate again and send her on her way. My father would not know if she was in calf until Sonny came to collect his fee of £1 ...

Once, we had to call the vet out at 3 o'clock in the morning because the cow had got into difficulty calving. Sadly the calf had died and the vet had to take the calf from the cow. The vet told my father to get rid of the cow as she would never be in calf again. My father didn't take this advice; the cow made a good recovery and before long had found her way to the bull again.

At the seventh month my dad could tell she was in calf again and we kept vigil on her day and night for the next two months. I remember the discomfort of my watch, as at that time I had my leg in plaster and was on crutches.

As is often the case in such matters, advice was freely given. One neighbour said to leave her on her own and she'd calve in her own time. Another said it would be tomorrow at the earliest – my dad didn't think it would be that night either. So, imagine my surprise when I hobbled out to the field the next morning and there was the cow licking clean two healthy twin calves.

I rushed as best I could to tell everyone else the good news and before long we were all walking into town – after a short distance it was evident that one of the calves was not quite as strong as the other, so, I leaned my crutches against a wall and carried the weaker one in my arms. What a sight I must have been to the neighbours, limping along carrying a calf.

***

This might make a little more sense if I tell you that my family were butchers. We had had a shop in the village since the 1860s.

Butchery practices were certainly a little different in those days to the present day. Meat would be hung on crooks outside the shop. When a heifer had been slaughtered, the head would be hung in the window with the tongue hanging out and the teeth exposed. This would indicate to those who knew, the age of the slaughtered heifer. Two teeth indicated the meat was from a two year old, four teeth would indicate a three year old beast. If she was more teeth than this ... well, the head would be left in the slaughterhouse.

Imagine just popping down to SuperValu for a couple of chops, only to be greeted by a severed cow's head dripping blood onto a sawdust covered floor ... we'd all be vegetarians. The next day the beef would be brought into the shop and displayed in the window. This would often catch the eye of the driver of the Westport bus, which would pass through Lanesborough every day.

He would stop his bus outside the shop and come in to talk to my father about the meat and other butchery matters. I think he was so interested because his people were butchers in Mayo. The old system of buying and selling has long since disappeared. We would visit the market in Ballymahon every month to buy one or two heifers.

When my father decided upon a suitable beast or beasts to buy, the first thing he would do would be to take little interest, almost ignoring them; if he did engage the selling party it would be to point out all the faults that the beasts had. This seemed to be an accepted ritual. My father would then point at a heifer and ask: "How much?" The farmer would probably say £40 and my father would turn and say £30 and not a penny more and make to walk away from the transaction, saying: "Come along John, we've a funeral to attend."

***

When the heifer had finally become our property she immediately changed into a prize-winning animal and all our neighbours attending the fair would be brought to see the wonderful animal and point out all the good points it possessed.

My father used to get a lift to the Ballymahon market with a cattle dealer from Roscommon. I would go on my bicycle. After the market was over I would walk the heifer back to Lanesborough and my father would return on my bike.

I vividly recall one spring day, I was working in the garden when we were both startled by a noise that sounded like thunder. I ran out into the street to witness a drove of about 30 or 40 cattle coming over the wooden bridge across the Shannon. I said to my father that one day I was going to own a herd like that and to hear them coming over the bridge would be music to my ears. I succeeded in my aspiration to own the cattle all right, but by the time I did the wooden bridge had long been replaced and the movement of cattle had become motorised.

There was one other service offered by my father's butchers shop, he could cure you of an upset tummy!

The following recipe would sort you in no time at all.

2oz Salts
2oz Sulphur
1oz Nitre – Potassium Nitrate
1/2oz Tarter
1/2oz Ginger (the weight of a shilling coin would suffice)
Mix the salts with the sulphur, then add the rest.
Take half a glass for two days then miss a day. *(YUK, Ed.)*

John with his friend Professor John O'Hagan, the son of one of Master Ned's eight daughters.

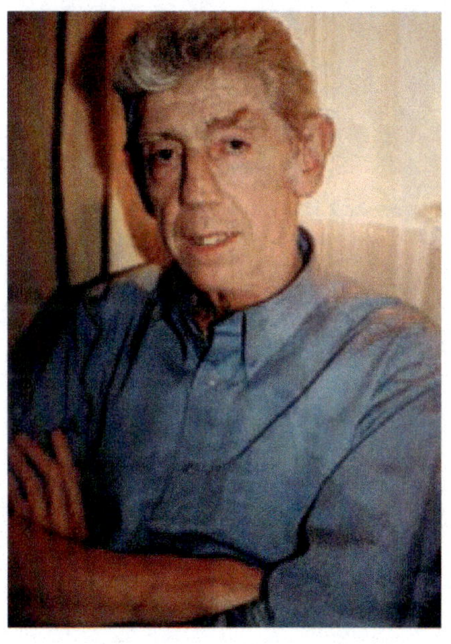

LEFT: Michael Mulvihill, John's co-worker at the butchers for forty plus years.

Michael was an extremely agree able and well liked man, who had a great rapport with many of the shop's customers.

Enterprising Shannonsiders

by Eddie Coffey

Plans for the creation of a large number of employment opportunities on either side of the Shannon at Lanesboro and Ballyleague were pressing ahead this week, as two separate groups planned for the future.

Last week a scheme was announced for the creation of at least fifty jobs in Ballyleague in 1989, with the creation of a mushroom village there over the coming months. This will be the culmination of months of study and voluntary work by a group of locals, interested in helping the community.

The Ballyleague and Rathcline Community Enterprise Groups are both on FAS-sponsored programmes and, like the mushroom village on the Roscommon side, the Lanesboro group are also planning the creation of an industrial base, work on which is due to commence in the coming year.

The Chairman of the Ballyleague group, Mr. Frank Curley told the LEADER that communities must now face up to the fact that unless they help themselves, nobody else is going to come and do the work for them.

● Fabian Walsh and Kathleen Kelly of the Rathcline Community Enterprise Group interview John Casey in Lanesboro. *Pic.: Joe McDonagh.*

Our 'enterprising author', pictured with the late Fabian Walsh and Kathleen Kelly.

CHAPTER

3

MEMORIES OF MY FATHER'S FORGE

by: Tommy Murray

My father, Jim Murray was the blacksmith in Lanesborough for three decades, through the 1930s, '40s, and '50s. In fact, right up until machinery replaced the horse as the main contributor to farm work. His forge was situated at the back of Ger Farrell's Bar and Grocery, now Lanesborough Tri-Club and Adie Farrell's Lounge Bar.

However, if cartwheels needed to be shod, my father would do this on the Green, beside the village pump. Shoeing a wheel involved fixing an iron hoop or tyre on the rim of the wooden cartwheel to support and protect the fellows (the part of the rim into which the spokes are inserted) to ensure a perfect circle for the wheel to turn on. Iron tyres or rims would occasionally come loose, particularly in hot weather, so the wheel would have to be re-shod. Sometimes, new tyres would have to be made when the old ones wore out or if a wheelwright had made new wheels.

At that time on the Green, several large chestnut and sycamore trees stood proud. My father had driven into one of these chestnut trees, three large metal spikes, close together and forming a triangle in shape. He

The craft of the Wheelright.

would then take a straight length of iron and, using the spikes, would shape a circle. He would then weld the two ends together to form an unbroken circular hoop. He would accurately measure the length of iron needed by use of a wheel disc. He would run the disc around the circumference of the wooden wheel, and then along the metal bar, measuring the bar just slightly under the wheel's circumference.

Whether making for a new tyre or re-shoeing an old one, the method was exactly the same. The wooden wheel would be sat on the shoeing stone. This was a large, circular concrete flag, with a hole or well in the centre to accommodate the wheel's hub, so that the spokes and fellows could lie nice and flat. Dad's shoeing stone was about 20 feet from the town pump, so there would always be a handy supply of water available.

The rim or tyre meanwhile would be placed on a few stones nearby. Around the rim would be sods of turf which would be lit and replenished until such time as the tyre was glowing red hot.

The rim would then be lifted from the fire with gripping tongs or 'dogs' and quickly placed over the wooden wheel sat adjacent on the shoeing stone. The great skill of the blacksmith would be to then sledge the rim onto the wheel while water would be poured onto the wheel to both stop the rim setting fire to the wood and also making the rim shrink to tighten its grip on the wheel.

As I became a certain age and, as the eldest son, I would become my father's apprentice on most of the shoeing jobs.

I would have my own pair of tongs and stand opposite dad picking up the rim out of the fire, at his signal it would be lowered as accurately as possible onto the wheel. I would then follow dad's sledging with a bucket of water, dousing and shrinking at the same time.

I can still recall the smells of the burning wood and the metallic odour of the cooling iron tyre. No matter how many times my father went through the process of shoeing wheels it would always be an attraction and gather a crowd, mostly it must be said from the kids of the village. Behind my father's back they would pillage lit sods of turf and start their own little fires all over the green, so much so that over the years large holes were burned in the nooks between the roots of many of the Green's trees. The trees were so big and well established these fires seemed to have no detrimental effect on them in any way.

When my father had returned to the forge it took the village children no time at all to take possession of the major, rim-burning fire, and it would be theirs for the rest of the evening.

Alas, these beautiful trees are no more, they were felled in the name of progress some years later. The old shoeing stone suffered the same fate.

***

My father's forge stood at the upper end of Ger Farrell's large yard, at the back of his pub and grocers shop, on the Rathcline road, just yards from the main street. Most of the time the interior was dark and gloomy, but there was a reason for this, as we shall see later.

Once a two story dwelling house, the second floor had been long removed and most of the windows blocked off. This resulted, I recall, in a most dark, gloomy and not a little spooky interior. There was no chimney flue as such and the smoke ascending from my father's work, with the aid of the draught from the open door, would exit through the remains of the external chimney block at the vertex of the roof.

At night my father worked in candle light or from the light of a hissing carbide lamp – electrification had not yet arrived in the village, with the exception of Dr. O'Halloran's wind-charger. The carbide lamp had two chambers, the bottom chamber held the carbide, and the top chamber held water which dripped down through a valve onto the carbide to create a gas that, when ignited, provided light as it escaped through a nozzle. A reflector behind the nozzle helped to project the light throughout the forge.

Carbide lamps were a very popular way of early artificial illumination. everything from lighthouses to street lights, early car headlights to even smaller versions for push bikes were widely used. they were also known as Acetylene Lamps as the chemical reaction of the calcium carbide and water produces acetylene.

An early Carbide Lamp.

To the left from the doorway to the forge stood Big Paddy Farrell's woodwork and construction workshop and, down the yard nearer the road on the same side was the pub's bottling store. Over this, on the second floor was the wool store where fleeces of wool were packed into large heavy bales ready for transportation.

Just outside the door of the forge was a large trough of water, an essential element of the blacksmith's trade.

Under the sole window to the front of the forge lay an old rusty plough much in need of repair, but long forgotten about by its owner who, in any case, may well have emigrated or passed to his eternal reward many years previously. To the right of the forge at the gable end of Big Paddy's house sat a mowing machine, in much the same state as the plough. Both, I'm sure, would have a provenance of a history of hard work, both would have seen good times and bad times and even the struggle for survival, sadly there would be no one to record or recount it.

From time to time other miscellaneous pieces of machinery would clutter up the yard, all waiting for dad's attention, and you could be sure, that invariably a few horses would be tied up at the front of the forge, patiently waiting shoeing. This provided a perfect opportunity for their thirsty owners to disappear through the back door of Ger's pub and wash away the dust of the day with a few pints and a bit of 'craic' before collecting their newly shod animals and returning to their farms and smallholdings.

The interior of dad's forge was made up of a few but essential pieces of equipment, all had their own importance but the **anvil** was the workbench where my father did most of his forging. The anvil was made from cast iron with a tool steel face which would not dent easily and had good rebound. It outlasted him for almost thirty years a blacksmith. It had two holes in its face, a round one and a square one for holding small tools.

The anvil is now an exhibit in Roscommon museum.

It was at this anvil that he forged the thousands of horseshoes that he must have made in nearly three decades. Just imagine the number of horses, ponies, mules, jennets and donkeys that would be active in Lanesborough and its surrounds back then.

It was at this anvil that he repaired and sharpened the coulters (cutting blades) of ploughs, or mended broken plough socks. It was here that he put new blades on horse drawn mowing machine cutters. It was this same anvil that made many dozens of gates for local farmers and households.

One prominent example that can still be seen is in front of the priest's house at Killashee. It is the small gate in the front wall, once used by pedestrians, right opposite the priest's front door. He told me some years later that he was never paid for making it! But then, he was used to that.

Of equal importance in dad's forge, or any other really, was the hearth or fire pit. This sat in the centre of a large circular built up containing bed of old ash and cinders to the outside, while fresher burning materials were fired toward the centre. He used coal and coke for fuel and sometimes turf clods to get the fire really going.

He would control the heat of the fire by use of large groaning **bellows** which fanned the fire to the required temperature. As children, we argued furiously as to whose turn it was to pump the bellows. One thing he never allowed was for anyone to stand between the fire and the anvil, for when he grasped the hot metal from the fire, in his tongs and swung round to the anvil, there could be a serious accident if anyone was in the way.

If the piece lost heat it was back to the fire and the bellows once more. This is where the semi-darkness of the forge came in, he could see more clearly the colour of the heated metal – red, yellow to almost white – which enabled him to judge better when it was ready to go back to the anvil.

Probably his most important tool was his **hammer,** or rather, his hammers. He had quite a collection as you might imagine. Smallish claw hammers mostly for shoeing horses, right up to great sledges that we kids could hardly pick up.

His **tongs** he would make himself and there was always a selection of **chisels and punches. I** recall them being labelled 'hot' and 'cold', hot for hot metal, cold for cold. The punch would be used for putting the holes in horseshoes.

All this would sit on or above a very strong **workbench** that was anchored to the wall, and attached to the workbench was an equally strong **vice.** He also had an instrument for threading pieces of iron and a box of dyes called a **Tap and Dye Set**.

These pieces of equipment, together with the water trough outside the door of his forge are the ones I recall most vividly.

Sadly, I don't think anything has survived from dad's forge other than the Tap and Dye set and the Anvil which was given to Roscommon Museum.

The lower part of the yard was equally busy and just as cluttered, with both full and empty porter barrels being delivered and collected by the lorries which ran on coal-gas.

There was a very large weighing scales to weigh the great bales of wool that was bought by Ger from farmers from both sides of the Shannon. Occasionally lorries would collect it in even bigger bales and take it down to the river to be loaded onto barges and taken further afield. A lean-to shed acted as a rudimentary urinal, a place best avoided whenever possible and there was even an outdoor shop-dump with a low wall where our Persian cat would gorge himself on out-of-date kippers or salted herrings and give himself 'mange' as a result of this overindulgence in a salty diet. This condition would result in immediate banishment from his cosy cushion beside the fire to the draughty corner of the open turf shed – an exile that baffled him, as you could tell from his plaintive meows, and his various efforts to break back into where he though he rightfully belonged.

***

The Man

My father, dad, or Jim the Blacksmith as he was more widely known, hailed from Kilteevan, just across the Shannon. He served a four year apprenticeship with Hanlon's Smithy in Ballymurray, and subsequently worked as a blacksmith in Athlone, Creggs and Roscommon town. He met and married a local woman, Mary Farrell from Lisnacusha, and settled in Lanesborough in the early 1930s.

By no means a big man, but he was broad shouldered and possessed great physical strength. He was a footballer of note having played with club teams in Kilteevan, Knockcroghery and Roscommon town. He also appeared for the county Roscommon in the 1920s. He was a fine weight thrower and won many trophies in this discipline at sports events and regattas throughout the region. I have a pair of vases that he won back in the '20s. Miraculously they survived, as his usual practice on such occasions was to give the trophy to the first acquaintance he met after the presentation.

Even in to his forties he could easily beat some of the local worthies at throwing the half hundred weight. I witnessed many a battle in the forge yard when some strong-man farmer fancied his chances and invited dad to take him on, always with the same result, victory for dad.

Ger Farrell, the pub owner, a hefty well-built man himself, was determined to beat him and time after time would challenge him, with the same result. All this was done with great banter and fun, and it was back to work for everybody when the contest was over.

Dad was a great story-teller and the forge would ring with laughter whenever the locals dropped by for a chat, or if a few local farmers were present. A hospitable man, and for those farmers who didn't retire to Ger's for a drink while waiting for work to be done, he would order tea and sandwiches or slices of fresh soda bread and jam. I would be dispatched home on this errand, and return with a full tray. Dad would take the tray from me and hold it out to the hungry farmer. My poor mother got little credit for this, but true to tell, she would have had it no other way, rather than to see a farmer go away hungry.

My father always warned us to take particular care around horses and instilled in us the greatest caution, and to be extra mindful when passing to the rear of any animal tied up in the yard. He pointed out to us that any horse, pony or donkey left standing in the one spot for a few hours without water or food could turn it into a mean spirited beast.

I was very lucky on one occasion when a horse belonging to the local egg buyer had been tied up for some time. The horse looked asleep to me and seemed totally unaware of my presence, but as I tried to slip quietly by, he lashed out. Fortunately, his kick had reached the end of its span before he caught me just behind the knee, and no serious damage was done. A quarter of an inch more and my knee would have been smashed.

***

Shoeing a Horse

Of all the tasks my father performed in the forge it was the shoeing of horses (or ponies or donkeys) that fascinated me the most. He seemed to have a hypnotic control of the animal from the time it came into the forge. He would have a whispered chat with it while stroking its nose and running his hand over its flanks. There would be occasional exceptions, but he would never allow us to stay in the forge if there was a flighty horse to be shod. I must have seen him performing this task of shoeing hundreds of times but it never failed to hold my attention.

The years have clouded the mirror of my memory, but the following is what I recall:

I can still evoke the combinations of sounds and smells that invaded the senses. everything from the asthmatic groans of the big bellows to the different bell-like sound ringing off the anvil as he worked at shaping the shoe. the pungent smell of coal smoke, the acrid burning smell of the horses hoof as he applied the hot shoe for a first fitting. I was always astonished that the animal felt no more in this process than I would with a broken nail. the metallic smell of the iron being cooled in the water trough and, on any occasion the animal decided to relieve itself, the odour of horse droppings. occasionally, my father's terse, staccato commands to the horse if he detected a little skittishness, the tapping of the hammer as the nails were driven into the hoof, and finally the sound of the rasp as my father trimmed and smoothed the newly shod hoof.

For the task, he had a small rectangular box with a handle, this contained all the tools he would need for the job. the box was always to hand as he moved from one hoof to the other in the hour-long task of a full shoeing. the box contained pincers, a shoeing hammer, a file or rasp, nippers, a hoof knife, a clinching block and, of course, a supply of nails.

It should be mentioned here that every time he worked at the animals hooves he would turn his back to the horse's leg in question, and take the hoof between his knees or, he might place the hoof across one knee and tuck his hip tightly into the horse's hock; in either position he would take the weight of the horse's leg.

The anvil is now an exhibit in Roscommon museum.

For a full shoeing dad would have to repeat this process four times and he wouldn't stop until he had finished the job to his satisfaction. Back-breaking work!

The work was tough, but dad was strong and used to it. Unfortunately, he wasn't always paid immediately, if at all, for his labours. I remember chatting with him many years later and him telling me that he'd be a rich man if everyone had paid him for his work. It was often a case of, 'God bless you, I'll see you after Mass on Sunday, but they never told me which Mass or which Sunday!'

At heart I knew he understood their position in the tough times of the thirties, forties and fifties, but in truth, our little family could have done with the 'write-offs' at times during this same period.

Despite the physical demands of his trade and the long hours he had to put in, dad still found time to milk two cows, rear a few weanlings, feed a couple of pigs, sow a few drills of potatoes and vegetables, save hay and make a hay-stack in the back garden and cut, make up and draw home a bank of turf – all in the way of keeping his hungry family fed and warm.

Just occasionally he might have had a little help from one of the journeyman or itinerant blacksmiths that regularly trod the boreens of Ireland in the twenties, thirties and forties. Many of these were experienced blacksmiths who travelled the country from smithy to smithy on the hope of a few days or even week's work.

If dad had a backlog of work on he would welcome such visits, but at other times if work was slack he considered them more of a nuisance.

I can recall a few of these travellers, many were very eccentric characters to say the least. One such individual we called 'hole in the hat' for obvious reasons and he hated children. No matter how friendly we tried to be he never once acknowledged any of us. He would sleep on a few sacks in the forge and eat whatever my mother sent out to him. Dad said that a lot of them were suffering from shell-shock they got serving in the British army in WWI.

They slipped away as unexpectedly as they had come, usually at night and having earned a few pounds. They wouldn't be seen again for at least twelve months, if at all.

The forge is no more. It has outlived its usefulness. It was demolished in the early eighties, along with Big Paddy's house to make way for an extension to Farrell's Supermarket.

When the forge work began to dry up with the advent of machinery taking over from the horse in the early fifties, dad took the changes with equanimity, and took a job with Bord na Mona, in charge of a small group of men assembling and laying tracks for the locomotives which traversed the local bogs.

The shoeing stone on the Green has long since disappeared, but a plaque to dad's memory can be seen on the edge of the Green, adjacent to the recently restored village pump.

Stop by and have a look, if you can spare a few moments.

CHAPTER

PAT FEE

Pat Fee was born in Killala, in the county Mayo. Around the year 1870 he came, as a young boy, with his mother to the Turlough, Parish of Rathcline.

Mrs. Fee was a "Street Singer" who could usually be found performing at fairs in Roscommon and Longford and any others close enough for her to get to. If a neighbour was selling sheep or pigs at a fair this usually meant she was sure of a lift home in the vacated crate. The poor woman had a bit of a weakness for the drink and often she would sing the whole way home from the fair.

Mrs. Fee would offer, if asked, that her husband was a soldier and had been killed in the wars. The neighbours built a hut for her, up near Johnnie Fallons on the Commons, there was a pathway into the Turlough there. There was a circus there, I think it was "Murrays", the same circus would put up at Rhattigan's garden, at the big house when we were going to school in the '40s. Times were very hard for the Fee family – Mrs. Fee would often spend much of her day begging for food. She died in Longford Poorhouse and was buried in the adjacent graveyard.

Pat Fee continued to live at the Turlough, his little hut had a bottomless bucket for a chimney. He had no furniture – only a stone to sit on in the hut and nothing but an armful of straw to sleep on – all in just one small room. He slept in his clothes and when they needed a wash he took them off and whacked them against a rock. "That will git the divilment out of ya," he would say. When Sunday arrived he would step out of his hut and face towards the chapel in Newtown Cashel at about the same time he knew the priest would be saying Mass. He sometimes mixed his words up, and as he knelt there, hands clasped together in front of him, he could be heard to say: "Our father who drafted into heaven" and "Blessed Michael the dark angel", "Blessed Mary never virgin" and many other such devotions. Father Greene, God rest him, used to say that the man who made the "offer" was as good in God's eyes as the saints. When Pat Fee died he was penniless, the neighbours looked after the burial. Michael Brennan's grandfather made him a coffin, and the boys carried him to Cashel graveyard. The night of his "wake" the boys had a gallon of porter, given by Lukey Farrell for those who would stay the night with Pat. A good number assembled on the night, and Pat, who had a hunchback, had to be tied down to a plank when he was "laid out". Some time later the boys were playing a game and John Connor and the boy Concannon, unbeknownst to the others, cut the rope, and ... "up sits" Pat Fee. Well, the hut cleared as fast as you can imagine, all receiving a great fright. But in no time at all the boys all returned, tied Pat down again and drank the porter.

In Cashel cemetery today you can still see and read Pats tombstone, which says:

FEE
Here lies Pat Fee of Turlough fame
Who died 4th March 1900.

CHAPTER

5

JIMMY MURRAY

Jimmy Murray was a native of Rathcline parish. In the year 2001 Jimmy turned 90.

There is a clock that hangs on Jimmy's kitchen wall that tells its own story ... or might do. When sharing a cup of tea and a biscuit with Jimmy one fine morning, John Casey enquired after the clock. Jimmy said that his father had bought the clock from a German travelling salesman in 1912. German salesmen were travelling the length of the country at this time selling clocks.

The idea was that they would return every two months to receive the next instalment for the clock payment. Jimmy's father said he was as delighted as any purchaser of one of these clocks because they never saw hair nor hide of the salesman after his initial visit.

This, of course, begs the question, was the clock selling just a ruse? Jimmy said it became the family's conviction, and many others like them, that these German salesman were actually "spies" who were mapping the Irish countryside, for a possible deployment of their forces who would then support any German invasion of England from these shores. It was subsequently proven that when WWI started in 1914, the Germans most definitely had plans to invade England.

***

Prior to WWI there had developed throughout Ireland, and other countries, a definite wariness about foreigners, especially those of a German origin.

There was considerable anxiety in local populations, enhanced by much scaremongering from the national press, that foreign agents abounded and were at work trying to weaken Britain's naval and military defences.

People began seeing "spies" everywhere, turning on neighbours and even turning to violence against anyone with a German ancestry.

CHAPTER

6

FR. JOSEPH MURPHY S.J.

You may recall from the second chapter of this book, John Casey's *Lanesborough Memories*, that there was a humorous incident regarding the arrival from America of a priest, John's first cousin.

This was Fr. Joseph Murphy, a native born American, but one who had strong connections to this area. He went on to touch the lives of many people, not only here in Ireland but all over the world.

Joseph was born in Philadelphia on 28th April 1911, the first-born of Irish immigrants, Patrick Murphy from Carlow and Elizabeth Casey from Longford. His mother had emigrated to America just two years earlier in 1909. To give an idea of the extent of emigration to America at that time, Joseph's mother was one of 228 Longford women who made their way transatlantic in that year alone. In the same twelve month period 252 Longford men made the same journey.

Fr. Joseph Murphy SJ.

Misfortune came early to the Murphy family and when only ten years old Joseph suffered the very sad loss of his mother, and Patrick the loss of his wife, mother now to three sons. Two years later Patrick married another Lanesborough woman – Bridget Killian, which subsequently resulted in a half-brother for Joseph, namely Daniel.

Joseph did well at school and progressed to a Catholic high school in 1925, graduating four years later in 1929. It was two years after this that Joseph made the significant and decisive decision to become a Jesuit priest.

Loyola University, Chicago.

The journey to becoming a Jesuit, or a member of the Society of Jesus, is a long and arduous one, involving both rigorous study and meaningful pastoral ministry.

Father Joseph entered the Novitiate of St. Andrew of the Hudson, Poughkeepsie, NY, on 30/07/31. He took his first vows after two years but then followed two more years study at St. Andrew. In 1935 he moved to West Baden College in Indiana. West Baden has quite a colourful history. The building itself is dominated by a large free-standing dome situated over the Atrium. In fact between the years 1902–'13 this was the largest dome of its type in the world.

The Atrium, from its time as a luxury hotel.

West Baden College was affiliated with Loyola University in Chicago and in 1938, having completed his Philosophical studies, Joseph graduated with an M.A. in English from Loyola University.

Following this period of his education Joseph was required to undertake fieldwork to prove his suitability for admission to the Order. He taught English and Public Speaking at Georgetown University. Georgetown is the oldest Catholic and Jesuit institute for higher learning in the USA.

It was certainly a long and meandering journey to the priesthood as Joseph, in 1941 and for the next four years, found himself at Woodstock Theological College in Maryland. The culmination of this journey of study came on the 18th June 1944 when Joseph was finally ordained as a priest by Archbishop Michael Curley, a native of Athlone.

Woodstock Theological College.

Once ordained and fully aware of the world situation, Father Joseph wrote to his superiors expressing a wish to be considered for foreign mission. He went on that he would also like to be considered for a military chaplaincy.

He wrote:

"If our men are then to be sent to countries, in any part of the world, which are short of priests as an aftermath of the war, please consider me as a volunteer also for this."

Also he added: *"If the Maryland province had a permanent foreign mission, he was happy to be considered."*

***

Father Joseph was not to get his wish granted just yet. Though he was to spend much of his life in the foreign missions, he was first assigned a role at the shrine of Our Lady of the Martyrs in New York. Following which he travelled to Rome for further doctrinal education at the Gregorian University there.

Back in the USA the church had other plans for Father Murphy and he was appointed to the staff of Woodstock College as a lecturer in dogmatic theology and only two years later became Dean of Theology.

Further advancements through the academic institution followed until, at last in 1957, Father Joseph got what he most craved, an overseas posting.

In 1957 the now Rector of Woodstock College was posted to become Rector of the Catholic Seminary in Rangoon, the capital of Burma. Burma was, and became even more so, a challenging ordeal,

Father Joseph was to undertake the re-establishment of the Jesuit presence in the country at a time when upheaval was in the air.

Subsequently, in 1962 there was a military coup in the country and all Catholics non-domiciled prior to 1948 were expelled. Father Joseph stayed in the USA for a few years before, in 1967 he moved to live in the Loyola House of Studies in Manilla, capital of the Philippines.

He found his new country also in a state of turmoil. Ferdinand Marcos had been elected in 1965 to counter the poverty and corruption that was rife in the country.

Father Joseph continued his vocation throughout the changes that were taking place not only in the Philippines but also in Catholicism, where it had been decreed, much to the displeasure of many in the priesthood, that the use of Latin be phased out for more vernacular language. Father Joseph battled on through these changes until, finally in 1963, he was given and accepted a sabbatical.

Father Joseph used this period of paid leave to travel to various Pacific Island groups like the Marshall and the Carolines, where he gave retreats and spoke at conferences.

Rather than returning to America, *"nobody there needs me",* he instead returned to Manilla, to a new home in the Jesuit residence on the campus of the Ateneo de Manilla University, where he adopted the role of Spiritual Father to the Community, still giving the odd lecture, and no doubt sage advice to the students.

There he lived peacefully until suddenly on Tuesday, 8th September 1987 he died at home in the Ateneo Jesuit residence. He was seventy-six years old.

CHAPTER

7

THE DOCTOR

This story was told by Joan McMahon *(Née Rhattigan)* who grew up in Lanesborough in the 1920s–'30s. She lived with her family in Clonbonny House.

I can picture him like it was yesterday.

I always thought our little village picturesque, a long wide street which started as a hill but flattened out as it reached the river. The village green was at the highest point, the road separating it from the Church, the School and the Presbytery. As you walked down the hill on the main street, there stood the General Stores. Nothing uncommon about that, every village had its General Stores, but in our case, it was the occupants, who were to say the least, unusual. The local doctor, our General Practitioner, our local character supreme, had his home there. To manage the store he had a most wonderful and kindly lady, a Miss Fox, whose smile never faltered despite having to co-exist with our eccentric and at times volatile doctor. This co-existence was purely platonic and of a business nature you understand, each following different paths away from the store. It was an extraordinary *menage a deux* – the practical and kindly shopkeeper, whilst lurking in the background our medical saviour.

He was the stuff of legend locally – as children we were terrified of him. He was very partial to strong drink and when under the influence was at his most venomous.

He wore silk dressing gowns, usually in a shade of maroon and he would stand at the door of the stores twirling his handlebar moustache, casting an unmissable shadow in that area of the street.

If sent on an errand you dreaded seeing him as you cycled onto the main street. As you cycled past he would roar: "you have a powerful pair of limbs", or something in a similar gist. When your errand necessitated an actual visit to the stores you would tremble at the knees, wondering what critical comments awaited you, but once past his towering frame in the doorway you felt safe with the kindly lady, who seemed completely immune to his eccentricities. He was, there can be no denying it, a brilliant doctor, but his methods were to say the least unorthodox. He had a very clever brain, which he kept in mint condition, always medically up to date and well read on every possible medical condition.

He delivered babies for miles around, but if called out in the middle of the night he gave vent to his displeasure and woe betide any poor woman in labour who had this extra worry to contend with.

Another astonishing fact about our doctor is that he was married ... for one night. The mind positively boggles at this piece of information, whatever could have happened that neither party was prepared to offer the other 'just one more night in the bridal suite'. But no, off our bride went the very next day to the nearby town of Longford, eventually opening a shop there.

And that was that ...

Mrs. McMahon finishes her piece by saying what a pity his deeds, and misdeeds, were not recorded for posterity, these are only the bones of his life, if we knew all of his exploits what a nostalgic tale it would tell.

***

Our Doctor, it transpires was born in County Clare in 1883, and the 1901 census shows him to be lodging at a house in Belvedere Terrace, Rotunda where, at age 18 he is a medical student.

By the 1911 census he has moved to Lanesborough where that year's census report shows him living at house 21 in Lanesborough town; also residing at the same address were two of his cousins from Co. Clare, namely Letitia Ryan aged 18 and her brother Michael Ryan then aged 22. Michael Ryan later played a prominent role in the

Republican movement, see *Troubled Times.*

However, further research of the said gentleman has revealed a number of other occasions where his activities became public.

This next piece echoes with much that has been said above – not a man to be messed with.

CENSUS OF IRELAND, 1911.

FORM A.

	Christian Name	Surname	Relation to Head of Family	Religious Profession	Education	Age (Males)	Age (Females)	Rank, Profession, or Occupation	Particulars as to Marriage	Where Born	Irish Language
1	Joseph	O'Halloran	Head of Family	R Catholic	Read & Write	28		Medical Doctor	Married	Co Clare	Irish & English
2	Michael	Ryan	Visitor	R Catholic	Read & Write	22		Cycle Mechanic	Single	Co Clare	
3	Lilian	Ryan	Visitor	R Catholic	Read & Write		18		Single	Co Clare	

I believe the foregoing to be a true Return.

Joseph O'Halloran, Signature of Head of Family.

LONGFORD LEADER 14/03/42

An application from Dr. O'Halloran, Lanesborough, for an increase of salary was adjourned, waiting for the attendance of secretary Mrs. M Brady who is on sick leave.

The clerk, (Miss C A Wilson) said she was telling the Board unofficially that Dr. O'Halloran had sent in his resignation since the last meeting, he then came in afterwards and took back his letter of resignation and put it on the fire.

Instead, he now wrote:

> "It has come to my knowledge that, after thirty-three years of service, instead of having one of the highest salaries of the *Medical Officers* of this county, I actually have the smallest, with no exception. I attach a list showing the accuracy of this.
>
> Surely, this is an extraordinary state of affairs, for I often wondered

did the new doctors coming on get as big a salary as mine, but I see that they start with a better one. Is this fair? Surely no, and I beg to apply for a substantial increase. Why? I am the doyen of the family in this county, with the exception of Dr. Yorke of Edgeworthstown. I beg that you will put this matter before the Board at its next meeting with a view to putting me on a par with the other Medical Officers."

The Clerk, (Miss C A Wilson) said, according to the list Dr. O'Halloran's salary of £230 per annum is the lowest, the other salaries being: Dr. M Farrell £285, Dr. O'Reilly £285, Dr. Coyne (Ballymahon) £285, Dr. Yorke £275, Dr. O'Mahony £255, Dr. Rhattigan £255 and Dr. Kirwan £250.

The Chairman said he understood the Board had fixed a scale of salaries. But he won ...

LONGFORD LEADER 18/04/42

DOCTORS SALARIES INCREASED

The adjourned application of Dr. O'Halloran MO, Lanesborough to be put on the same salary scale as other dispensary doctors came up for consideration.

In his application Dr. O'Halloran pointed out that after thirty-three years of service instead of having one of the highest salaries in the county, he actually had the lowest.

The Chairman understood that since the Board came into effect in 1934 they had a fixed scale for all Medical Officers, it was also noted that Dr. Yorke of Edgeworthstown was also being paid outside the scale.

On the proposition of Mr. Carter and seconded by Mr. Belton it was decided to put both Dr. O'Halloran and Dr. Yorke on the scale.

Footnote by editor: An increase from £230 to £285 per annum would today equate to about £3,000.

***

A good few years earlier than the above events, our illustrious doctor was involved in quite a serious motor accident, surely an event more rare and unusual in those days than now.

It was reported by the *Longford Leader*, Saturday, 13th August 1938:

"While motoring to the Leinster Hurling final at Tullamore on Sunday week, Dr. JA O'Halloran, Lanesborough, met with a serious accident. It appears, when approaching Kildare Cross, seven miles from Mullingar, the driver of the car was forced to swerve to avoid a collision with another car coming from a side road. The car colliding with a wall and immediately bursting into flames. Luckily one of the car doors flew open with the force of the impact and Dr. O'Halloran and the driver, although both injured, were able to get out of the car with the aid of Miss B Fox who was also in the car.

A car was hastily summoned from Mullingar and the injured people travelled back there to hospital. Dr. O'Halloran suffered spinal injuries and severe bruising but we are glad to learn that his life is not in danger. The driver of the car, Mr. Peter Elliot had several ribs fractured, whilst Miss Fox suffered from a sore back.

It was most providential that the car door flew open or they would have all been burned to death, as it was the car completely burned out in a very short space of time. During the past week numerous calls have been made as to the well being of Dr. O'Halloran who is extremely popular with all classes.

The other car involved in the accident was also completely burned out and the driver, Mr. Gallagher, an accountant from Mullingar, also suffered fractured ribs."

***

A slightly more amusing tale relating to Dr. O'Halloran was again reported by the *Longford Leader* earlier the same year. This was regarding a court case:

In Longford District Court, before Mr. J P Kenny D.J., Patrick Farrell of Moher, Lanesborough, was charged as follows:

Firstly, that on the 12th of February he did unlawfully, wilfully and maliciously commit damage to a glass panel of a door, the property of Dr. J A O'Halloran, Lanesborough, whereby he sustained £1 loss.

Secondly, that he damaged a sleeping bench in the Barracks, the property of the Commissioners of Public Works, the damage being estimated at 15/-.

Thirdly, that he was guilty, while drunk, of disorderly behaviour.

Dr. O'Halloran gave evidence that on the 12th February, (fair day in Lanesborough), Patrick Farrell, the defendant, rushed into his premises. He was being held by a couple of companions, including a first cousin. He created a scene and was obviously very drunk. He made a glancing kick at the witness. The two men pulled him out of the shop and when passing the door made a kick at it and broke a glass panel. The damage caused by the defendant would be about £1. Since the summons was issued the defendant paid him £1 compensation for the damage.

Justice: "Was his conduct very bad?"

"Yes."

Justice: "Did he use bad language?"

"No, there was a strong man in the street bending nails with his teeth and lighting weights, and he went over to him and jolted up against him a couple of times."

"He was a dangerous man to hit up against," remarked the Justice, amidst laughter. Dr. O'Halloran said he thought he'd been drinking Brandy that day.

Then added: *"A thing I didn't take myself for twenty years."*

Justice: "It was necessary to do that to look at the man eating nails", (more laughter). The defendant, Patrick Farrell, came forward and said he'd settled with all the people concerned.

Justice: "With whom? The man that was eating the nails? What did you do with the man that was eating nails?"

"He frightened me sir."

Justice: "Is that why you went to the doctor?"

"No, I went for cigarettes, when I was going out the glass fell out of the door..." (more laughter).

Justice: "What made it fall out?"

"It was cracked about three months before."

Justice: "What cracked it?"

"The witness could not say," replied the witness.

Guard O'Brien, Lanesborough, gave evidence that the defendant's conduct was such that he had to take him to the barracks.

"He was drunk and disorderly and had damaged the door in Dr. O'Halloran's at the time."

The Guard said it was necessary to put him in the lock-up.

Guard Brady gave evidence that while in the lock-up the defendant started to kick the door. With the assistance of the Sergeant he took the boots off the defendant. Later, when Guard Brady went back to the lock-up the defendant had damaged the sleeping bench, the Guard added that when he went back later the bench was completely smashed. The damage done to the sleeping bench was estimated at 15/-.

In reply to the Justice, the Guard said that the defendant did not get drunk very often, but he and his father did not agree. The defendant added that when he sat down on the bench the boards went down under him (more laughter).

Justice: "That was in the cell?"

"Yes."

Justice: "The cell wants repairs!"

"It does sir." (laughter).

Justice: "Well, have you paid for the repairs? You know there is 15/- due."

"But, do you see, I paid some and they gave it back to me, and I spent it", (more laughter).

Justice: "Who did you give it to?"

"I left 2/6 in the barracks for the repairs and gave Dr. O'Halloran £1, I got the glass panel examined and it was only worth 5/-".

Justice: "So the doctor did well."

"He did sir."

"What about the 15/- for the repairs in the cell?" asked the Justice.

"Well, I am financially embarrassed," claimed the defendant amidst much more laughter.

Justice: "When do you think you will be able to pay the 15/-?"

"Ah, I don't know sir."

Justice: "If you facilitate me in that way then I shall facilitate you in another, but if you do not, things are going to be serious".

"Well, would you think sir, that the boards were worth 15/-?" asked the defendant. Justice: "Not being in your position, I cannot say." (laughter)

"Well, now supposing a glass case that you would buy at 2/6 would do all the repairs?"

Justice: "I am afraid this is all getting too complicated", (more laughter).

In respect of the charge of damaging Dr. O'Halloran's premises, the defendant was let off with a caution.

On the charge of damaging the cell, the defendant was fined 5/- and 15/- compensation. The defendant was cautioned in respect of the drunkenness charge.

Supt. O'Dowd said expenses amounted to £1 11/- being 10/- for a car and £1 1/- for Dr. O'Halloran's attendance.

"This is becoming serious," said the Justice.

Memorial Card of Dr. Joseph A. O'Halloran.

The text above doesn't read quite as straight - forwardly as it might today, but I have reproduced it how it was reported all those years ago.

CHAPTER

8

THE DAVYS FAMILY

Even in a country with 60,679 townlands it is not all that common to have one named after a living family, more often than not they are geographical descriptions taken from old Irish.

The townland of Mount Davys lies just to the east of that of Clonbonny, which in turn gives its name to the house occupied for so long by the Davys family.

In that excellent local history work, *"Pathways to the past – Rathcline"* family member Lewis Rhattigan gives a brief history of the Davys family, using for much of his source material, the actual Davys Family Records, chronicled by various family members from 1693–1832.

These original record books and diaries were uncovered by a family member, at a much later date in the offices of a Dublin solicitor. These records were then prepared for publication by S F Ó Cianáin M.B. (J F Keenan) a local historian and presumably medical man who wrote about a number of prominent midlands families.

The bridge at Portadown.

They were indeed published over five consecutive weeks from Oct 10th – Nov 7th 1931 in the *Longford Leader*.

What remains something of a mystery is how the Davys family, at all times staunch Catholics, remained so relatively affluent after the Penal Laws were introduced to Ireland, both before and subsequent to, the 1641 rebellion.

The 1641 uprising or rebellion in Ireland, remains one of the most brutal and bloodthirsty events to ever happen here. The uprising hoped to return confiscated lands to the Catholic aristocracy, proposed greater self-governance, and an end to anti-Catholic discrimination.

That it was brutal is beyond refute. At Portadown as many as 100 Protestants were thrown off the bridge into the river Bann; they were then shot as they tried to swim to safety. At Islandmagee in Co. Tyrone, two dozen Catholics were murdered by members of the Carrickfergus garrison.

There are many, many examples of atrocities carried out by both sides, in fact historian of the rebellion, William Lecky, wrote: *"It is far from clear on which side the balance of cruelty rests."*

As a result of this rebellion and its aftermath, later that decade Ireland was to receive what became known as the Cromwellian Visitation.

By the end of this particular dark chapter of Irish history, Cromwell had ensured that almost all Irish land was in the hands of Protestants.

However, not so the land and property owned by the Davys family.

It would be fascinating to learn more of the politics of the time, with specific regard to the Davys but alas, though the records kept by the family are incredibly detailed and informative, they refer in the main only to family matters.

In the modern vernacular, Matches, Hatches and Dispatches are listed with great fervour, chapter and verse, but nothing is much written about outside events, and virtually nothing of a political nature.

What follows are just a few details from the records where other events have been documented.

***

The first of the Davys of whom we have a definitive record is that of George – he died on May 2nd 1696 and was buried in the old Catholic graveyard of the Abbey at Lanesborough. This is now St John's Church of Ireland parish church.

In earlier times the Abbey had been a Preceptory (community and buildings) of the Knights Templar.

The Knights were formed circa 1119 and were a military order of the Catholic faith.

Records suggest that the site of the present day St John's has been a place of worship since Christianity first came to Ireland in the early 6th century.

***

Another thing which did concern the Davys chroniclers was the weather. *(Nothing changes.)*

The Davys family residence, sold to John Rhattigan in 1904. The sale included 550 acres. Photo by kind permission of Breda Walsh.

It is noted that the Shannon froze completely across in 1740, 1776 and 1784, and at other times.

Also recorded at the same time as the above, though no specific date is given, is the collapse of the Tower of the Dominican Abbey in Roscommon, I would imagine quite an event in its day. The Abbey was founded in 1253 but the tower wasn't added until renovations were made in the 15th century.

***

Another more poignant entry.

"Monday, February ye 2nd, 1702 happened ye woeful accident at Lanesborough, when were drowned in the pontoone 35 persons, 11 more having escaped, among which I was one, Richard Davys."

***

More disastrous weather:

"Decbr. 30th 1739 – the great frost began with a violent storm which destroyed all the potatoes in 24 hours. The Shannon was frozen across tho' ye stream was great, and ye 1th and 2th o January there was great snow. Men and horses crossed ye Shannon on ye ice and several carriers and bullocks, and both snow and frost continued till

ye 28th of Feby.

And then on parching winds without one drop of rain till ye 1th of August 1740, which made a scarce harvest."

Then later:

"The great snow began Jany ye 4th 1745 and continued till ye last of February, and ye 11th march it began again and kilt more sheep than ye first, which left few behind as it was so deep, and yet left few black catell or sheep in ye kingdom."

Editor's note: If we suffered these kind of weather conditions today it would all be the fault of global warming!

***

In the month of March 1753 disaster struck the Davys family which had commercial repercussions:

"March ye 11th, 1753 N.S. – Sunday, 9.00 o'clock at night, my stable (at Clonbonny) with 4 saddle horses, cow house, barn, malt-house, kills, haggard and hay, with 300 barrells of oak-bark, was burnt to ye value of 8 or 900 lbs. [sic] occasioned by a candel that Daniel Gibelan, a poor scholar in ye house for 5 or 6 years, took with him to goe to bed, which would be burnt but (he) was dragged off; and bless god none was lost or hurt, and dyed 14 horses to may following and 900 sheep."

Then in May 1753:

"May 1753 – Last spring there was a general rott of sheep, where I lost nine hundred. my brothers children lost eleven hundred and ye country in proportion, which ris wooll 10/- to 12/- per stone and continues to the year 1692, sold from 10/- to 11/9 which was gott at Balnaslow for mine and childrens and Mr. G Taaffe's childrens' 40 bags."

(Evidently this last part was added in 1762 by George's son James.)

Editor's note: Oak-bark was used in the process of tanning skins and hides.

***

In 1775–'76 there followed more family tragedy and desperate weather conditions:

"Oct, 19th 1775 – Mrs. Catherine Ferrall alias Davys, her two daughters and son Francis, drowned on the coast of Wales."

"1776 Jany 4th – Began a frost which continued to the 30th Jany,

rotted many potatoes and the Shannon was frozen across."

Winter 1784:

"Jany 16 – Began a violent storm attended with frost and snow which continued to the 20th Feby. The Shannon was frozen for almost the whole time. Horses and carts drew turf from Connaught to Fermoyle on the ice. No potatoes in ridges or holes rotted, many in houses."

***

On April 3rd 1790 the following was recorded:

"My house and offices in Flax Park Roscommon, with 18 other houses in the town, burned by a timber Lanthorn on a malt-kiln taking fire belonging to Francis rue."

***

"1795 April 26th – two large cocks of hay, 70 ton, burnt at 12. o'clock at night in the Church Park at Grange by the 'Defenders', worth £120, set out for only £85. Same night broak my three doors which were to the barn of Cloonmurley, stripped most of the barn of thatch, spread the greater part of a large haycock out in the fields, broak the walls and pens there, cutt some Ash trees, went from thence to the grove, levelled down several perches of walls, broak two gates, and cutt seven Ash trees in both places."

Here we have perhaps the only entry in the entire records of what might be described as political in nature.

The Defenders were a Catholic Agrarian Secret Society whose main focus in life was to oppose the Protestant Peep o' Day Boys. (The Peep o' Day Boys evolved into the Orange Order)

Defenders were also active against Landlords and their agents, which is why the property of the Davys family would have been attacked.

Made up mostly of poor Irish Catholic rural workers, they were formed in response to the miserable conditions most tenant farmers and rural workers lived in in the late 18th and early 19th century.

Later in the early 19th century they became known as Ribbonmen, the name being derived from a green ribbon worn as a badge in a buttonhole. Another name by which they had come to be known was Threshers.

On the 22nd January 1814, William Davys, Captain Lanesborough Infantry, penned two letters to (we assume) his senior officer – we don't have this officer's name as the letters are addressed to Major...

These are reprinted verbatim:

First letter:

Dear major

The Treshers (Captain Davys refers to them without h in their name) came into this parish last night and I believe some of them across the Shannon on the ice; that it seems from Corporal Kelly's statement – who I send to you to give every information as they broke into his house and took a small gun from him. I wish you would again write to government to allow a Sergeant Guard for the protection of our arms. I wish the entire Corps were put on duty, if but for one month, that we may be out every night as lately this part of the country is in a very alarming state.

I remain dear Major very truly yours.

Wm. Davys

Second letter:

Sir,

Enclosed you have the examinations of Corporal Kelly of my Corps, and since I wrote to you this morning I find that a different party of those Treshers went to the house of another member of my Corps, who lives in Leghery (but one mile and a half from this) to demand his arms but he got out a back door and called assistance on which they made off. I fear unless some active steps are instantly taken this part of the country will be in a very bad state as from the hard frost the disaffected in Roscommon can at this time join those in this part by crossing the Shannon on the ice, but you may rest assured that we are determined to give them a warm reception should they once more attack Lanesborough.

I have the honour to remain Sir

Your obedient and very humble servant,

William Davys Captain Lanesborough Infantry.

***

Just a few years before the above events the 1798 Rebellion took place in Ireland.

The records read as follows:

"1798 Sept. 8th – A battle fought by the French and the rebels, who joined them, between our army and the above, at Ballinamuck, Co. Longford."

One of the Davys clan took part, or nearly did.

"William Davys was captain of the Lanesborough Yeomanry and marched with his company to Ballinamuck, on the report of the approach of the French, but arrived there, it is said, the day after the battle".

This gentleman, say the records, was described as:

"Very dashing, extravagant and fashionable. He was a grand Juror in 1796".

Wolfe Tone.

This battle and its aftermath gives us another example of the brutality of the time. A total of 96 French officers and 746 men were taken prisoner, British losses perhaps 12. Approximately 500 French and Irish lay dead on the field. 200 Irish prisoners were taken in mopping up operations, almost all of whom were later hanged, including Mathew Tone, brother of Wolfe Tone. The prisoners were moved to Ballinalee where most were executed in what is known locally as Bully's Field.

***

The records aren't entirely clear which member of the family recorded the next section, though it may well have been Christopher Davys.

"1818 Aug. 24 – the first prisoner confined in the new Goal [Gaol] of Roscommon was Owen Cumane, of Ballymurray, Co. Rosc. He was confined in the old Goal for Rioting several times, and when in confinement there he commenced great turbulence and mutiny by breaking a door and burning it and stirring up the other prisoners to mutiny.

Old jail, Roscommon.

Application being made to me by John Carson – Under Sheriff, and Joseph Heily Governor of the Goal, I committed him to solitary confinement in the new Goal".

***

It is interesting to note from the records, that certainly in the earlier years, not only were deaths recorded but often the manner of the passing recorded.

A number of unusual episodes stand out.

It was not uncommon for death to be recorded as, "Fell off a horse".

Another term used quite frequently was: "Died paralityk", this would mean paralysed and so of a stroke.

"Dropsy" was another relatively common cause of death. Dropsy was a term used for many centuries to define a syndrome of fluid overload, and signified congestive heart failure. One of the most common entries refers to "Died of the Gravel". Somewhat ironically.

Gravel was an accumulation of Kidney Stones.

In the later years of the diaries just the fact of someone's passing is recorded.

What a wonderful source of information well kept diaries are to the historian. they so knit together the minutiae of everyday life through the years. (Ed)

CHAPTER

9

TWO WHO TRAVELLED

Throughout most of the 19th century and early 20th century, travel to distant lands was but a dream for the vast majority of people. There will have been many people in those years who lived and died without leaving even the confines of Lanesborough or neighbouring townlands.

Then, as now, two surefire ways of seeing the world were to either join the Army or the Priesthood and apply for foreign missions.

JAMES McDERMOTT

Born in 1786 or thereabouts in the parish of Clentuscart in or near the town of Lanesborough in the County of Roscommon, James joined from the Roscommon militia, His Majesty's 87th Prince's Own Irish Regiment of Foot, 2nd March 1808.

(*His service record goes on to say):* Promoted to Corporal 11th July 1809, prisoner of war March to June 1810, promoted Sgt. 25th April 1811, in the peninsula until about July 1814. (The Peninsular War 1807–1814 fought on the Spanish/Portuguese peninsula against Napoleon.)

Sailed for India in January 1818 to join 1st Battalion Captain Goate's company, Cawnpore, Calcutta 1821 until July when on the Ganges for Dinapore, reached in August: In November at Ghazipore to Rangoon where he rejoins the regiment.

In February 1826 promoted Sargent Major and transferred from Coatio to Carroll's company in June. In hospital July and August, back on duty September, at sea October to Calcutta - November 1827. At sea February to June, invalided to Fort Pitt Chatham. July pensioned.

Examined by the Chelsea Hospital Board and admitted to pension 3rd September 1827, age 41.

Served 18 years 1 month as a Sgt., 1 year as a Cpl., and 1 year as a Private. Served in East Indies 8 years 11 months, entitled to extra services = total services 24 years 6 months. Pensioned at 1s/2d a day. Reason for discharge 'Worn Out'. Height 5'7", brown hair, grey eyes, fair complexion, conduct very good. Military General Service Medal with 8 clasps. Talavera, Barossa, Vittoria, Pyrenees, Nivelle, Nive, Orthes and Toulouse (all actions in the Peninsula War).

According to ecclesiastical records at the India Office Library, James McDermott was a widower when, on the 10th September 1821, he married by banns Mary Anne McMahon, a widow; both are given as "of the garrison Fort William, Calcutta", and they were married by the garrison chaplain.

What Sgt. Major James McDermott might have looked like.

According to the muster role, by September 1821 he was at Dinapore. There is no record or details of his first wife. As his wife, Mary Anne McMahon would have returned to Ireland with him, free of charge.

James McDermott died in 1858 aged 72, he is buried in Lanesborough Cemetery, his Tombstone reads:

"James McDermott fought with distinction in the Indian Wars. Died 1858 aged 72. His son Charles, died at New York in 1862 aged 28 years of wounds received in the American forces."

What Trooper Charles McDermott might have looked like.

Editor's note: it is interesting that James was honoured 8 times for his service in the peninsular War, but his tombstone only mentions the Indian Wars.

Unless further evidence comes to light we must assume his son Charles emigrated to America around the time of, or just before, his father's death. It would appear he died fighting for the Unionist Forces in the American Civil War.

Adjutant Anthony W. McDermott who wrote the short initial history of the 69th.

Coincidental to the above about Charles, the picture below shows Adjutant Anthony W. McDermott (we believe no relation), who also fought in the American Civil War.

Anthony was born in Gortgallen townland Cloontuskert, Co. Roscommon. He served in the 69th Pennsylvania Veteran Volunteers. After the war he wrote a brief history of the 69th Penn. Vet. Vol. He died 15th May 1916 aged 75 and is buried in the Old Cathedral Cemetery, Philadelphia.

FATHER LARRY LEAVY

The parish of Rathcline is noted for the number of priests it has given to the Catholic Church. However, few families in Lanesborough can match the record of the Leavy family who have given no fewer than three priests to the church.

Father Larry Leavy was ordained in Maynooth and in 1935 sent to minister in Nigeria.

The following letter, dated Weds Oct 2nd 1935, was sent to his mother en-route.

Dearest Mother,

This day week we were knocking around home and now we're getting into the heat of the tropics. We're getting on near the coast of Africa having passed by the Bay of Biscay and the coasts of Spain and Portugal. tomorrow we expect to call into the port of Tenerife where I will post this.

It surely seems to be a dream more than a reality – all that has passed within the last few days. I didn't properly realise what was happening until we left Liverpool and found ourselves out at sea. It goes without saying that I was lonely. I kept picturing you and the old home to myself and wondering how you both were. Are you alright? Remember you promised me you would take a rest and go to bed in time. Don't you or J.P. be worried or lonely – I don't regret my decision one bit, in spite of hard partings. We are just soldiers for Christ and soldiers must take their orders and do hard things.

Srs. Ignatius and Teresa came to Liverpool to see us off, also Fr. Barry. they were the last glimpses of Erin we saw. uncle John or Fr. Ryan will have told you of the crowd who saw us off at the north Wall. I'm very glad indeed J.P. didn't come to Dublin. I wouldn't have stood a chance of speaking to him satisfactorily and I would have been properly fed up.

The voyage is very nice, the boat is good, though it is only a large cargo boat. There are however seven passengers on board as well as ourselves and we have very comfortable quarters. The food and the attendance is just perfect. The ships officers are all very courteous – they even call us "father" which is unusual. All of us were sick except Tommy on Sunday and Monday. I wasn't too bad but had to keep lying down or I'd be in a bad way. The ships on this line are shallow and consequently roll a good deal. We have a gramophone with us and among our records we have

McCormacks – several of them, Frank Lee's Ceilidhe Band, and listen – "Kelly's cow has got no tail".

When we get into real good form we propose to have a few songs on deck ourselves – Irish ones of course. Due to the rolling I haven't been able to say mass yet. Tommy said Mass twice, but he had no aftermath of sea-sickness to get over. Tomorrow however, the feast of our dear patron – The Little Flower – I'll say Mass or die in the attempt.

We have of course been out of sight of land since last Sunday, so there's nothing interesting to write for a few days. oh yes! The other night the purser invited us to his wireless and we heard Athlone, one item on the Programme was a hornpipe on the pipes. We were somewhere off the Spanish coast at the time and weren't we glad to hear a voice from home.

Don't you like that send-off on Sunday morning. Fr. Camillus was charmed with it. I think the poor lads in the band were fine to turn out the way they did, led of course by big paddy with "de hairs on his legs". He is a good sort. It won't be long till they're out to welcome us home again.

I'm writing to Fr. Ryan, sally, Agnes and a few others from the boat. you'll hear from me again on the sea. I have nothing else to do but write. I will let you know the mail days when you can write to me. "Catholic Mission, Calabar, Nigeria" will find me any time. Fr. Ryan will give you any information you require on the matter.

Now I assure you I'm alright and very happy. Your cheerfulness last Friday meant a lot to me. May God reward you for it and may he take care of you both till we sail again for dear old Erin.

Your loving son Larry.

A sad end to Father Leavy's mission, sadly he died in Calabar, Nigeria just fourteen months after writing that letter, in December 1936.

The Headstone reads:

Sweet Jesus have mercy on the soul of Rev. LAURENCE.J.LEAVY, Lanesboro, Co. Longford, Ireland. Who died at Calabar, 27th December 1936. In the 26th year of his age And the 2nd of his Ministry. R.I.P.

CHAPTER

10

MICHAEL CASEY CRAFTSMAN

Michael Casey was born in 1932 and was destined to join the generations of Casey butchers like his brother John. However, Michael was a free spirit, a wanderer and for him the less travelled path of carpentry beckoned.

Carpentry stole Michael away and within that trade and particular skill he could satisfy his wanderlust.

Helping Hands, Mullingar Hospital.

Michael first took his skills, in 1950 to England, travelling from city to city where there was no shortage of work rebuilding a country devastated by the second World War. Five years later Michael found himself on a boat out of Cobh bound for Canada. Travelling down the St Lawrence, first to Montreal for a year, then on to Toronto. The wanderlust returned, Michael forked out $100 on an old Chevrolet and what followed was the road trip of a lifetime, Chicago to San Francisco. Michael loved San Francisco and there was no shortage of work there, but slowly, over time, the little town of Lanesborough and the rolling woods of Rathcline, coupled with missed family, started to tug at his heartstrings.

In 1962 Michael gave £25 for a little field close to the Shannon in Newtowncashel. Here he built a studio and later a home and has been there ever since.

Even as a child Michael loved wood, the smell of it entranced him.

"There was a carpenter's shop close to where I lived, and on the weekends I discovered a secret way of getting into it. I used to enjoy smelling the wood and just touching it – the red deal and the white pine – and planning it. I had to go out by the door, I'm sure he must have known that something was going on, but he never said anything."

The Dancer.

In the years after returning to Ireland, Michael did any kind of carpentry that came his way. He built a couple of Gypsy Caravans, one of which he kept for himself for his excursions into Connemara.

It was through the caravan that Michael met his wife. He put an ad in *the Sunday Times* and a young woman from the Netherlands named Elly answered it. *"She came over and rented it and that's how I met her."* They married in 1968 and their son Kevin was born in 1969.

His first real work of art came about almost by accident. He had started to work on a piece of bogwood when suddenly a form began to emerge from the shape of the wood itself. He called the piece *the dancer,* he says it was in some way a response to the work of the late Barbara Hepworth, whose untimely death he had been reading about in *the Irish times.* Michael still has this piece and it's one he will never sell.

Michael admits that he had never really looked at Art books, but he felt a kinship with Hepworth and her remarkable wood sculptures – a feeling reinforced when he visited her home and workshops at St. Ives in Cornwall.

He discovered another kindred spirit some years later when he visited the Museum of Modern Art in Paris. There, he wandered into a room where the studio of the great Romanian wood sculptor, Brancusi, had been reconstructed.

"I don't think I was ever as excited in my whole life as I was seeing this studio, his soaring birds became an inspiration to me and I suppose my herons are a response to them".

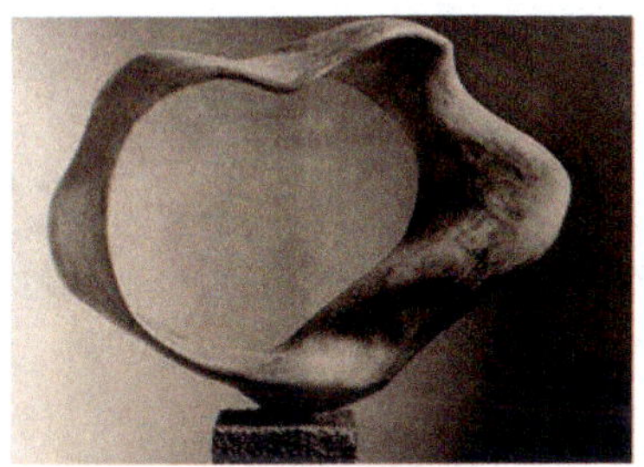

Cloud With Light.

One of John's Herons is seen by many of us on a daily basis, sitting as it does on its red buoy, eyes forever searching the river, just below the bridge on the Lanesborough side. For 50 years plus now Michael has been carving and engineering exquisite pieces of art from this natural material that is many thousands of years old. Finely detailed and refined, Michael's work has graced some of our finest institutions, it can be seen represented in Mullingar Hospital, in the Mater Hospital in Dublin, it has been gifted by the Irish government to Nelson Mandela no less.

One of the more spectacular of Michael's sculptures can be seen at the Trackway Centre at Corlea, where his depiction of 'Cuchulainn and the Horse' gives an immediate sense of gravitas and archaicism to the display.

On left is a depiction of **IR,** son of King Milesius, a powerful chieftain of the area. Created by Michael Casey who was fascinated by the story of a prehistoric ruler who is believed to be the forerunner of the O'Farrell Clan.

Over the years Michael Casey's art has been recognised and appreciated as some of the best of its type in the world. Indeed, one might ask what have Nelson Mandela, Bill Clinton, Yasser Arafat, Seamus Heaney, Ian Paisley, Charles Haughey and Pope John Paul II all got in common – the answer: these and many more, at one time or another, have all been presented with works by Michael Casey.

Noel Dempsey TD making the presentation to His Excellency Sheik Ahmed, Dubai.

Albert Reynolds making the presentation to Nelson Mandela.

Albert Reynolds making the presentation to Yasser Arafat.

Dermot Mannion, Aer Lingus, presenting Ian Paisley

Presentation of one of Michael's works of art to Seamus Heaney.

Longford's 'own' Taoiseach, Albert Reynolds is on record saying: ***"It pleases me very much that Irish people now have the confidence in their own heritage that they can present a gift of Irish Bog oak to a head of state or a prominent person".*** **Mr Reynolds continued:** ***"When I was starting off it was a different case, people seemed to think that anything local was not important – it's a sign of the changing times and a growing confidence."***

CHAPTER

11

JIMMY'S CLOCK

(We have no exact date for the next piece but it was written by Mairéad O'Shea)

As one of the oldest men in the parish of Rathcline, ninety-one years old Jimmy Shea of Blenavoher has witnessed many changes over his lifetime but one thing that has remained stable over the years is the ticking of the ancient clock which hangs in his family home, dating back to an incredible 1840.

The ancient family heirloom has hung in the Shea household since the early 1960s when Jimmy's late uncle John Shea brought the clock from his former home in the Roosky area.

Dated 1840 the clock appears much like a grandfather clock without a case. With its swinging pendulum and heavy weights it must be wound every day. Despite its incredible age of over 160 years, old Jimmy testifies that the clock has never stopped since it first entered the house back in the mid-'60s and in fact the only problem it presented was a worn out axle which was duly fixed.

Jimmy's uncle John Shea married a widowed lady from the Roosky area in the early 1900s who was known as the widow McManus. It was understood that the clock had remained in the McManus household in

Killglass, Roosky, over the years but following the destructive storm of 1847 it was blown to pieces as Jimmy explained.

"The great storm of 1847 blew the clock right off the wall and the pieces were gathered up and put in a box for years. It was only when my uncle John married the widow McManus years later that he found the clock, and being very handy with things like that was able to put it back together again."

John Shea was a native of Inchenagh Island and had lived in Dublin for many years before returning to Co. Longford and eventually marrying the widow McManus in the early 1900s. When John's wife died he returned to Blenavoher and lived with his nephew Jimmy, bringing the clock with him to the Shea household. The clock came into the house sometime in the mid- '60s and it has never stopped since, other than when Jimmy had to replace a worn wheel.

The clock figures had obviously dated and faded over the years resulting in Jimmy pasting a new face onto the clock some years later.

"You could hardly see the original figures so I pasted a new face onto the clock, but the date was there on it as 1840. I suppose if you scraped the new face off you'd be able to see the old one, but I didn't really think about it at the time, it's only years later you begin to place a value on something like that."

So, has Jimmy ever been tempted to part with the ancient clock?

Years ago these two men travelling the road came into the house and they offered me £50 for the clock, but sure I said to them, "What good would £50 be to me if I didn't have the time of day!" I wouldn't sell it to them, and I hardly will now at this stage.

The loud tick of an ancient clock is somewhat comforting, readily identifiable and is now firmly established as part of the Shea household.

As Jimmy said: "If I didn't wind the clock every day and I came down to the room in the morning, I'd miss the sound of it."

CHAPTER

12

TRIBUTES

Here John Casey pays tribute to two local men who both died in 2019.

A tribute to John Killian (1932 – 2019) John Killian was a lifelong farmer in his native Fermoyle but had retired to the town shortly before his death. Over the years he found time for sporting and cultural activities and performed with distinction in many local am/dram productions.

John had a wise view of life and a witty turn of phrase, which characterised his writing, both poetry and prose. At his funeral, Father Michael Reilly PP described John as a poet and a philosopher. I knew him as a philosopher more so than a poet. I would visit him weekly for about three hours and the conversation would cover a wide range of topics. We would talk about farming and the price of cattle, or should I say the 'bad' price of cattle. So to get a rise out of John, I would say, "But we are only hobby farmers anyway!" His reply would be, "You might be a hobby farmer

John Killian performing as Robert Emmet in the 1966 Pageant, 'A NATION ONCE AGAIN', commemorating the 50th anniversary of the uprising.

but I am NOT!" We talked about folklore and history, the ghost and the banshee stories that would be told by the old people long ago in rambling houses. The rambling houses in the parish of Rathcline were, as everywhere in Ireland, numerous.

It was a time in the not too distant past, when many people believed in fairies and many thought that they saw ghosts.

It was a time when neighbours in rural Ireland gathered in local farmhouses at night, and around the fireside discussed the simple events of the neighbourhood and told stories. The advent of television put an end to the visiting and storytelling, but the 'rambling house' will revive memories of those times for people who lived through them and may well give later generations an idea of what rural Ireland was like in the middle of the twentieth century.

It was a tradition that will not be seen again. Perhaps a piece like this will show generations yet unborn, a glimpse of the way of life lived by their ancestors and give future historians an insight into the peculiarities and customs of their forebears.

Hallowe'en

The land is bound up in a beautiful haze,
Like a picture on television portraying a dream,
The sun is the backdrop, throwing shades of light.
A nip in the air – there'll be white frost tonight.

The haze grows deeper, and i
Sit on an old stile to get a better view
Of the lake that's like glass. There's magic.
The stile is never used now: covered in moss,
Once the busy thoroughfare of fairies and commuters,
Now the seat of dreams.

The haze grows deeper and deeper.
The old woman with the red shawl appears in the distance.
She wanted me to talk to her once but I was afraid.
Now I want to talk to her, but she's too far away.
But I will.... tomorrow is the day.

The haze grows deeper, the crowd gets bigger.
I know them all – 'no names no pack drill' he said.

If they'd only stop and talk to me,
I'd have so much to say,
But I can tell it to them tomorrow,
Because tomorrow is All saints day.

John Killian died on All Saints Day 2019, he was the last of the storytellers of the parish of Rathcline.

May the good Lord look kindly on his generous soul.

Luke Kenny (1931–2019)

Luke was a classical scholar, self educated and a lover of poetry, both national and international.

One of his favourite poems was from the *oxford Book of American Verse* entitled 'The Song of Hiawatha' by Henry Wadsworth Longfellow. This poem is about an Indian chief but Luke always referred to them as Native Americans or indigenous peoples, who were badly treated by successive American governments in the 19th century.

In 1830, the U.S. Congress passed the Indian Removal Act authorising the government to relocate Native Americans from their homeland within established States, to lands west of the Mississippi river, which were marginal lands. This resulted in the ethnic cleansing of many tribes with brutal forced marches coming to be known as the 'Trail of Tears'. As many as four thousand of the Choctaw tribesmen, women and children perished when they were bullied out of their ancestral homeland and forced to cross the Mississippi. In spite of their own awful plight, when they heard of the Irish Famine in 1847, they subscribed the sum of $170. So, in honour of Luke Kenny, I would like to include two excerpts from *'THE SONG OF HIAWATHA'* :

Should you ask me whence these stories?
Whence these legends and traditions,
With the odors of the forest,
With the dew and damp of meadows,
With the curling smoke of wigwams,
With the rushing of great rivers,
With their frequent repetitions
With their wild reverberations.

There are longings, yearnings, strivings,
For the good they comprehend not,
That the feeble hands and helpless,
Groping blindly in the darkness,

Touch god's right hand in that darkness
And are lifted up and strengthened;
Listen to this simple truth,
To this Song of Hiawatha!
Ye, who sometimes in your rambles
Through the green lanes of the country,
Where the tangled barberry-bushes
Hang their tufts of crimson berries.

Luke also liked to talk about the European wars, both ancient and recent. He would mention the names of the major players, their mistakes and their achievements. He was steeped in the lore and traditions of his native place. He would talk about our culture and our heritage: the ploughing of the fields with his two horses in the month of March; the wide open spaces; the coming of the swallows; the fruits available on our hedgerows for our bees, birds and insects.

Unfortunately, the machine has taken its toll on our hedgerows and reduced the food for our wildlife.

Just as I was about to leave from one of my weekly visits, out of the blue he made an unusual comment. He said, 'A man should not leave the parish for a wife', I asked, 'And why is that Luke?' 'Tradition an Respect', came the reply – a statement from a confirmed bachelor if I ever heard one.

In farming families, the match left little room for individual choice – particularly for women. These were very formal, often unromantic bargains. Property and money were the important features of marriage. The attraction of a woman with a dowry! The actual values of a dowry varied with the status and means involved and might range from a few household items, such as pots and pans, sometimes a bed, up to significant cash sums.

May the good Lord look kindly on his generous soul.

Written in 2016, twelve months after his passing, Tommy Murray here pays tribute to another outstanding local Teacher, Poet, Playwright, Actor, Naturalist and Writer.

Seán Cahill (1931–2015)

Seán was born in Kilmacannon near Newtownforbes in 1931. He and his two brothers and two sisters enjoyed an idyllic upbringing with freedom to explore and discover the surrounding countryside.

Seán's first appearance in Lanesborough would be to visit Olive Gallagher his wife to be. In the same year they got married, 1956, Seán became principle of Fermoyle School. Pupils soon found themselves treading the boards and performed with distinction, particularly in Dublin, appearing at such venues as the Capuchin Hall and the Players-Wills Theatre.

There had been a long tradition of adult amateur dramatic theatre in Lanesborough, dating back to the 1930s. Seán soon became involved as a producer to many of the performances staged. In 1959 he and Fr. Jimmy Beirne CC produced a double bill of the plays *'RIDERS TO THE SEA'* and *'Boolavogue'*. In 1964 and 1965 Seán produced two of Agatha Christies's great stage plays, *'TEN LITTLE INDIANS'* and *'WITNESS FOR THE PROSECUTION'*.

A highlight of the sixties, however, was the 1966 Pageant, *'A NATION ONCE AGAIN'*, co-written and produced by Seán to mark the occasion of the fiftieth anniversary of the 1916 rising.

It traced the history of Irish Republicanism from 1798 to 1916, culminating in the truce of 1921. Dramatic scenes were enacted on stage relating to, Father Murphy, Robert Emmet, the Famine, the Fenians, planning the Rising, the taking of the GPO and the later arrival of the Black and Tans. Song and recitation were interwoven with the dramatic episodes.

"GREATER LOVE THAN THIS"
(A PASSION PLAY)
(By LANESBORO' DRAMATIC SOCIETY)
in
LANESBORO' HALL
Opening
SUNDAY, MARCH 23
ALSO ON
WEDNESDAY 26th, FRIDAY 28th and SUNDAY 30th
Doors open 8 p.m. Play commences 8.30 sharp.
Seats - - 4/-
(or Bookable at 5/- by phoning LANESBORO' [illegible])

More productions followed but the grand finale of the sixties was a Passion Play, *'NO GREATER LOVE'* which was written and produced by Seán in 1969.

The 1969 Passion Play — John Hyland, John Casey (author), Gerry Crean, Gabrielle Farrell (née Kelly), Tommy Murray (on the cross), Mary Gallagher, unsure, Hilary Sullivan and Jimmy Casey.

The cast of the 1936 Passion Play which includes Tommy Murray's mother playing the Virgin Mary.

The Passion Play 1936: Back Row (l-r) – Lewis Rhatigan, Alfred McCrann, Charlie Rhatigan, Johnny Connaughton, Ned Dempsey, Tom Gilhooly and James Casey. Second Row – Mrs. M.J. Daly, Mr. Hannan, Tom Hynes, Mike Martin, Bridie Higgins, Mrs. Mary Murray, Mrs. A. Glennon, Mrs. M. Rhatigan, Mrs. B. Leonard, Joe Flaherty and Mrs. Ena Farrell. Front Row – Seán McGettrick, Kitty Lyons, Joan Walsh, Peggy Rooney, Alice Hickey, Geraldine Ryan, Nancy Healy, Bridget Connaughton and Anthony O'Flaherty.

It was a moving and dignified performance, and, for some older members of the group and audience, brought back memories of a Passion Play, staged by members of the Lanesborough Dramatic Guild, thirty-four years earlier in 1935.

Seán Cahill.

In his early years Seán was a keen fowler and loved to walk the bogs and lowlands with his dog in pursuit of a pheasant or partridge. He soon noticed the declining numbers of these gamebirds and decided to do something about it.

He and a few friends were instrumental in having the Game Council of Ireland set up, with a view to preserving and increasing the population of these beautiful birds. He became particularly involved in the rearing of pheasants and partridges in captivity, releasing them into the wild when they reached a certain age.

The 'Newtownforbes' Project' was successful, especially in relation to pheasants, and there is no doubt that this, and similar projects elsewhere, made a large contribution to the survival of the species.

In his later years Seán expressed some regret that he had ever lifted a gun to these magnificent creatures.

After a period of living in Lanesborough Seán, Olive and their young family moved into a new house in Ballyleague, overlooking Lough Ree.

The Cahill home gained a reputation for hospitality, with always a warm welcome for neighbours, friends and casual callers. Sadly the tranquility of the household was shattered in 1984 when, after a short illness, Olive died.

This left Seán broken-hearted and facing the reality of caring for a young family on his own – a task he undertook with complete dedication.

Seán was a brilliant local historian who kept a sharp eye on the ancient sites and settlements of Lough Ree.

There is evidence to suggest that the ancient church in Rathcline cemetery once housed a monastic cell and had close connections with the monastic settlement on Inchcleraun. In 1990 Seán noticed that the eastern gable with its large tracery window was in danger of collapse. He and a few like-minded people initiated a project to secure and restore it.

Seán was also an active member of the Lasrai Writers Group to which he contributed many wonderful pieces of prose and poetry. He spent much of his time in his later years researching with his friend Jimmy Casey, and others for the book *'Rathcline – Pathways To The Past'*.

This work was followed by: *'Primary Schools In County Longford'* in 2000, *'Tell Me Shawn O'Farrell'* in 2002 and *'Lough Ree And Its Islands'* in 2006.

Seán was a deeply spiritual man with a practical faith and a relaxed and easy relationship with the Church and his God.

He had lived in Ballyleague for close on sixty years until ill health forced him to sell and move to a smaller, more self-contained home in

Tarmonbarry in 2009. He was greatly missed by all his friends and neighbours from both sides of the river, who held him in high esteem. He rests beside his beloved Olive in Rathcline Cemetery.

May the good Lord look kindly on his generous soul.

CHAPTER

13

I HAVE OFTEN WALKED DOWN THIS STREET BEFORE

by: Alan Jay Lerner – My Fair Lady

(The piece / title isn't by Alan Jay Lerner — AJL wrote a song of the same name in My Fair Lady, I have stolen the title as a pun)

In July 2013 I was asked by Christine McDonogh if I could give her a brief historical account, as I could recall it, of the residents of the Rathcline of my youth.

Christine recorded our conversation and gave me the following transcript. *(JC)*

During my teenage years there was only one house in the townland of Knock and it belonged to Kate Kelly. Kate was the Church bell-ringer and she rang the Church bell twice a day, at 12 noon to herald the Angelus and at 6.00pm in the evening. She would also ring the bell before the Sunday Masses. In those days there was an 8.00am Sunday Mass, a 9.30am Mass for visiting priests and the late Mass, as it was called then, at 11.30am. Kate rang the bell twice before the 11.30am Sunday Mass, firstly at 11.15am and for a second time at 11.25am.

Kate was a single lady who helped the large families of the town with their chores and laundry. She also cleaned the barracks for the local constabulary, but was bullied by some unsavoury characters to stop her from continuing this work. After ignoring their bullying tactics, they cut Kate's hair to frighten her.

Present house on Kate Kelly's site.

The site of Kate Kelly's house which was demolished to build the one now standing there. In later years this was the home of John Killian.

The next resident on the left hand side, coming into town on the Ballymahon Road was Elizabeth Cline, and she was also an unmarried lady. Her home was the first house beyond the church on the far side, where Iveta's Barber Shop currently is. Next door to Elizabeth Cline's house lived Elizabeth Maguire, she too was unmarried and was the grand aunt of Joe O'Brien.

Elizabeth Cline's house.

In the next house lived John O'Sullivan, a master tailor and the father of nine children. His small terraced house was home to his family and his tailor's business. His son Hillary lives there to this day.

John O'Sullivan's house.

Tom Gilloolly lived in the house next to John O'Sullivan. He was the local carpenter and builder and had two children. Dr Walsh's surgery is currently established in this house.

Tom Gilloolly's house.

The Harold family occupied the next house. They had a grocery and hardware shop, but also sold bicycles and radios. The family also owned the public house across the bridge in Ballyleague called Harold's Pub.

Mr Harold had three grown sons when I was a boy. Harold's had a system of Hire Purchase for the purchasing radios and bicycles. A system of 'Bailing' existed in those days, whereby a person of sound financial means went 'guarantor' on behalf of the person asking for the hire purchase item and loan.

The Harold's house.

James Murray lived in the house where currently the Gala Supermarket is and he was the local blacksmith and his forge was situated at the rear of the house where the current funeral home is located. He was a married man with five children.

The Murray house.

Ger Farrell lived next door to James Murray and he ran the pub, hardware and grocery store which is still in business to this day. Also, a Wool buyer and provider of undertaker services. Ger's son Adie, and Adie's son Gerard, continue to run the family business between them along with Josephine who runs the Gala supermarket.

Adie's premises.

On the same side across the road on the corner lived Pat Carroll who was the local postman and his home is where Joe O'Brien's shop is now.

Joe's father Jimmy bought the premises and opened his business, which is the present business now run by Joe and Martina O'Brien.

Pat Carroll's house.

It's worth remembering that John is talking about his youth but in 2013, so his 'now' references are over 10 years old. (Ed)

Where the take away chipper shop is, now owned by Seán Mimnagh, that was previously owned by Edward Kelly and he had a bicycle shop and a cinema at the rear where Dr. Ali's surgery currently is.

Premises previously owned by Edward Kelly.

Next door was the residence of Dr. Joseph O'Halloran, (See chapter, The Doctor) who came to the town in 1910. A married man, he built a two story house next to Edward Kelly's house. He operated his GP surgery from the house at that time.

He opened a hardware and grocery store however, what was written above the door was 'The General Supplies Stores Ltd' as he couldn't put his own name over the door due to the fact that he was a medical practitioner. He also opened the first Chemist shop in 1945 and hired a qualified chemist to manage it. It was later taken over by Orla O'Brien's father and aunt. He was also the trainer of the Ladies Camogie Team back in the 1930s. He died in the 1950s.

Dr. O'Halloran's.

Next door to Dr. O'Halloran's was Clarke's Pub – a well-known and historic public house established in 1824.

The Clarke family also ran a dairy and they farmed extensive land around the town. The milk for the town was supplied by them.

Clarke's Pub, established in 1824.

Next to Clarkes was the O'Flaherty residence. Originally it was a bakery set up inside a long thatched house but the O'Flaherty family built a large two story house and they extended their business to General Hardware, Grocery and Furniture, and dealt in anything and everything.

Anthony O'Flaherty and his wife Mona both ran the business, Anthony's father came originally from Strokestown. The O'Flaherty's business was based where Samantha's Bed and Breakfast is now.

Next door to the O'Flaherty's business premises was, and still is, Larry Leavy's home and business premises. Larry is a monumental sculptor and they have had monumental sculptors in the family for the past 150 years. The Leavy's and their ancestors have erected monuments over a wide area from Clonmacnoise to Drumshanbo Cemeteries.

Larry and his nephew Eamonn still run the business to this day.

After Leavys, the next four houses were part of a Stone Cut building scheme, built by the landlord Luke White, while across the road on the far side eight identical houses were also built. These replaced old thatched homes and were a considerable improvement to the look of the town of Lanesborough.

Luke White was a good and fair Landlord and lived in a large estate in Old Rathcline.

In the first of the Stone Cut houses lived Tom Scally. He ran a small business and had a petrol pump, a taxi service and a small confectionery shop.

James Casey lived next door to Tom and he had a butcher shop which was started by his grandfather Joseph Casey around 1912. *(James Casey would be a second cousin of mine. At one time there were six Casey families, by no means all related, living on Main Street)*

James Casey premises.

Where the current SuperValu supermarket is, this was formally the site of two of the Stone Cut houses, one of which was occupied by three General Practitioners, Dr. Moran, Dr. Donohoe and Dr. Condon, from 1945–2000 approx.

In the fourth lived Peter Mulleady and his wife Bridget, they ran a confectionery shop, petrol pumps, a car mechanical service and also a taxi.

In the next house lived Michael Duggan and his sister Rose. They ran a tailoring business in the early part of the 20th Century. Michael died when I was a young boy and the house was later demolished. The current car park for SuperValu is where Michael's house formerly stood.

The first premises just past the SuperValu was a monumental sculptors business run by Thomas Farrell, a business that stretched back to the 19th century. When I was a boy, Fabian Walsh ran a bakery business on the same site and later, Phil McGarry ran his engineering business from here.

Former Thomas Farrell premises.

In the next large house was a long established General Grocery and Hardware store run by the O'Connor family. Malachy O'Connor was married and his son Charles O'Connor fought at the battle of Ballinamuck in 1798. Charles fought and died for the cause of Irish freedom. After the battle, Charles body was retrieved, by his family in the dead of night, and interred secretly in Lanesborough old cemetery.

While Charles death occurred on September the 5th, which was the date of the battle, the date inscribed on his headstone was August to avoid any retaliation towards his family. He was only 21 years old at the time of his death and his family line died out

at the end of the 19th Century.
Ellen Farrell inherited the house from the O'Connor family whom she worked for. Ellen opened a small sweet shop which she ran until she passed away in the 1950s. She left the house to her nephew Michael Connaughton. It is now Pings Take Away.

The former O'Connor premises.

In the nineteenth century the next house was a Court House. (See chapter: Like a Scene from the Wild West.) This house later became the residence of the Catholic Curate. It is now the Shannon Cut hair-dressing salon.

Formerly a courthouse and curate's residence.

Again, John is talking here in 2013....

The next house is the only three story house in the town, this was built by John Costello in 1805. John was a General Merchant, a wool buyer, he had a boat hire business, horse drawn cabs for hire, hotel and post office businesses. John was also secretary of the Ballyleague Famine Relief Committee, and treasurer to the Famine Relief Committee in Rathcline.
On his cemetery headstone in old Rathcline, there is an epitaph to his generosity and goodness to the poor of both parishes during the famine years. His business died out with his passing in 1857.
The next occupier was Mary Jane Casey who continued to run the Post Office. Eventually the Post Office was taken over by Patricia Kelly, the mother of the present owner, Joe Kelly.

Premises built by John Costello in 1805.

Next we have St Mary's Parish Hall. This was built as the

barracks for the RIC in approx 1830. The barracks was operational from 1830 to the formation of the new state in 1922. It then became the premises of the newly-formed police force An Garda Síochána. The new Garda station in the townland of Knock was built in the 1950s. The premises were then handed over to the Parish of St. Mary's, Rathcline.

The Irish War of Independence has been fully researched by John and is in the Archivist section of Longford Library for safekeeping.

A story he loves to recount is as follows: *'My mother and father, before they were married, were walking along by the banks of Lough Ree, and my mother was wearing a red coat. the land was farmed by the Gill family and a large bull spotted my mother's red coat and charged at her. A young Black and Tan out walking his small terrier, set the dog on the bull and the bull changed direction, so no harm was done.'*

On the other side of the street in Lanesborough directly across from St. Mary's Parish Hall, the house where Bridie Holmes fish n' tackle shop is, was built by the four Donlan sisters, early in the 20th Century. Ellen, Mrs. De Pas, Mrs. Kelly and the nurse! The nurse was the maternity nurse for the parish and her name was Margaret. Mrs. De Pas and Mrs. Kelly returned from America and spent their remaining years in the house. It was eventually taken over by their niece Nancy Brennan. Nancy ran a confectionery shop and she was the first to sell ice-cream in the town when electricity was introduced.

Formerly Nancy Brennan's confectionery shop.

The next building was a very large premises. It ran from Nancy's shop as far as the Bank. In the 18th Century it was a brewery run by the Lewis family. It was alleged the family were Quakers. Early in the 19th Century it was taken over by the Davys family. Their country residence was Clonbonny House. They were a Loyalist Catholic family who farmed around a thousand acres but, they were no Landlords. The McCrann's took it over in the early part of the 20th Century. They were General Merchants, Wholesalers and Dance Hall proprietors. This large hall is still in operation today, *(2013)* and used for many local events. This building was eventually taken over by the Sisters of Mercy in 1954. They opened and ran a girl's Secondary Convent and Boarding School up until the '80s. Today the Lough Ree Co-Op Resource Centre operates from this building and the local Bridge Club play their weekly Bridge games there. Other organisations hold their meetings and events here also. The large dance floor is still there to the current day.

Currently Lough Ree Co-Op Resource Centre.

The former Northern Ireland Bank Building is next. Work on this building began in 1919 and was completed in 1922. At that time the English government were broke after WWI, so they targeted the banks for funding but the Northern Banks found a loophole to avoid paying funds to the government so they went on a building spree. They began building banks in Fermanagh, Carrick-on-Shannon, Elphin, Strokestown and the last bank at that time was built in Lanesborough *(I have more history on the bank, not listed here).* Gareth Johnson has his Pharmacy there now.

Formerly Northern Ireland Bank building.

Mark Shields had a premises next door to the Bank. Mark ran a small engineering business and sold spare parts, he also sold and repaired boat engines and lawnmowers. Formerly these premises had been owned by the McGuinness family who had a forge on the site from the 19th Century to the middle of the 20th Century. The remains of the old rooms of the forge could still be seen when I was a boy. The next building which is where the Lough Ree Arms currently stands was formerly the site of two stone cut houses of eight, these were identical to those over the road. The Lough Ree Arms Hotel was originally started by Rose Shannon from her stone cut house. Rose lived in the second house and Tom Kelly lived in the first and ran a small grocers shop from it. Both houses were eventually bought by the McNally family in the early 1950s. They incorporated both houses into the Hotel and subsequently opened the hotel's first public bar. Also, the hotel ran a garage with petrol pumps. The Lough Ree Arms Hotel ran as a business successfully until the late '90s. In the years following it was run by various proprietors until it eventually closed its doors due to the economic recession.

The former Lough Ree Arms hotel.

The next original stone cut house was owned by Terence Farrell who were renowned monumental sculptors. The members of their extended family built monuments in places like Trinity and various churches in Dublin. The history of the extended Terence Farrell family has been recorded and published.

Formerly Terence Farrell monumental sculptors.

In the fourth stone cut house which is gone from the site today lived Ms Dolan who was a teacher in Fermoyle National School. Today on this site is a lovely flower garden owned by Paddy and Anne Green.

In the fifth stone cut house lived and was previously owned by James Gahern who was an uncle of Paddy Green. The Gahern family were the original tenants of this house. The house was inherited by James' nephew Paddy Green, who still lives there today with his wife Anne.

The next house is currently owned by Frank Regan, auctioneer. Previously it was owned by Kathleen Kelly who ran a successful restaurant. Before that it was owned by the Leavy family. John and Elizabeth Leavy ran a busy drapers shop from here.

Formerly restaurant owned by Kathleen Kelly.

The drapers shop was later run by her daughter Kitty and her husband Bernard Moore until it was sold to Kathleen Kelly.

From 1929 was Casey's butchers premises.

Next was Casey's Butchers. The Casey family were also the original tenants of the stone cut houses. The butchery business was started by Daniel Casey in the latter half of the 19th Century. It was then passed on to his son Michael, then, Michael senior passed it on to his own son Michael *(my father)* who then passed it on to me, still the current owner of the building. The stone cut house was modified in 1929 as a butchers shop premises. *The history of Butchery and the meat trade has been recorded by JC but remains un*published. The remaining stone cut house which is next to the butcher shop is also owned by JC, who lived there for nearly forty years with his wife Mary. They raised their family there until they moved out to Gurteengar in 2007.

The previous owners of this house were Garda Joe Gallagher who raised a large family in this house. Before him Sergeant George Foley of the Royal Irish Constabulary lived here.

According to tradition the next house is one of the oldest premises in the town. From the early 20th Century it was owned by Seadna Ryan's family, who ran a successful grocery, hardware and garage stores. It has been owned by various people over the past recent years. It is alleged that in the 18th Century, a Revenue Police

Barracks operated from the premises.

Previously owned by Seadna Ryan's family.

Next door is a public house owned by Joe Farrell and his wife Martha. Joe and Martha have been running the business The Yacht Bar for at least thirty years. This premises was originally built by John Casey (no relation) around 1860. According to tradition it was built on the site of the old town drinking pond. Before the time of Joe Farrell it was owned by three other proprietors and was always run as a public house and grocery.

The Yacht Bar, owned by Joe and Martha Farrell.

Across the road on the far corner was also a stone house and it was owned by Adrian Farrell's family in the late 19th and early 20th Centuries. Back then the Farrell family business was as monumental sculptors.

Stone house formerly owned by Adrian Farrell.

In the next house lives Padraig Farrell and his mother Mary. It was originally owned by the Mulvihill family who farmed locally.

Padraig Farrell and his mother Mary's house.

The next house was the home of the Smith family. The family still own the house to this day as their ancestors have for over two hundred years.

The Smith family premises.

The Shanley family from Killashee lived in the next house. Originally this property was owned by the Church of Ireland in the 19th Century.

The house next to the Shanley's is owned by the Bannon family. In the early part of the 20th Century this house was owned by Patrick Farrell who ran a Saddlery business from it.

The Bannon family house.

The final house, where the library currently stands was owned by the Gaffney family and previously to that by the Bennett family.

This completes the record of houses, businesses and owners of the houses on the main street of Old Rathcline and Lanesborough. As I remember it from my youth...

As mentioned above, 'Joes'- the Yacht Bar was built by a John Casey, but prior to Joe Farrell taking on the pub, it was known as Casey's Corner Bar and the landlord was one Thomas Casey (again no relation). Local car enthusiast and petrol-head, Michael Connaughton, has provided us with some fascinating historical information.

The cars are pictured below…

This is the actual 1930 Austin, Reg No. 1X1043, that Thomas Casey bought from the Longford Arms Motor Works. Sadly for Thomas, he fell seriously ill just after this purchase and the car was hardly ever driven but garaged in a shed at the back of the bar. The car was eventually sold by Mr Jim O'Leary, a mechanic from Ryan's Garage, to a Mr John Doris of Longford.

Mickey tells us that the car then somewhat went off the radar, until many years later when sold by a man from Dublin to somebody in Glasson, then on to somebody in Mayo. It now resides, to the best of our knowledge, with an owner in Abbeyshrule.

Such was Mickey's interest in cars, that he made a note of all the cars and registration numbers of some of the more prominent local people.

Above is a 1935 Ford, similar to this model were cars driven by: Alfred McCrann, Pete Mulleady, Anthony Flaherty, Miss E Farrell, Thomas Fitzpatrick, Pat Clyne, P.J. O'Flaherty and Michael Casey.

A 1935 Swift, similar to that driven by Thomas J Kenny of Fermoyle.

A 1929 Citroen was driven by Father Goodwin.

John Harold drove a 1931 Essex and also a 1929 Ford.

James Farrell of Lisnacusha drove a 1931 Morris Cowley.

All of the above cars had an IX prefix to their number plates. IX was the identification lettering (from 1903 to 1970) to show the car had been registered in the County of Longford.

Michael has also told us where you could fill up the above cars.

P Kenny Garage – Brand CALTEX
Pete Mulleady – MEX
McNally's – ESSO
Tom Skelly – LOBITOS
Ryans – BP & SHELL
John Harold – CALTEX

We are indebted to Michael for the above information.

A MISCELLANY OF EVENTS, GEOGRAPHY, ARCHITECTURE AND OTHER HISTORICAL HAPPENINGS

CHAPTER

14

THE HUNT FOR LINCOLN'S KILLER

One of the consequences of the Great Hunger, was the huge numbers of emigrants that sought a fresh start and a new life in the Americas. As a consequence of this, there was suddenly a lot of fresh faced, fit, young Irishmen, living in the United States in 1861, when the US Civil War broke out.

One such Irishman who not only survived the slaughter, but rose through the ranks was Major James O'Beirne. James was only a boy when he was taken from Ballagh, Co. Roscommon, to New York, by his parents, Michael Horan O'Beirne and Eliza Rowan. *(We believe this to be the Ballagh between Ballyleague and Roscommon, though there is a smaller townland named Ballagh in the south of the county.)*

James was well educated at St Francis Xavier and St. John's colleges in the city. On completion of his studies he went to work in the offices of his father at Roche, O'Beirne & Co. After a short period, James had decided to go into business for himself but, before these plans could come to fruition they were interrupted by the outbreak of the America Civil War. In 1861 he enlisted as a private in the 7th New York National Guard, before joining the 37th New York Infantry, known as "The Irish Rifles". He joined as a 2nd Lieutenant but by the time of the Battle of Chancellorsville in May 1863 he had risen to the rank of Captain. At Chancellorsville he was seriously injured, a bullet had ripped through his right lung and he was also struck in the right leg and head. At the time it was feared his wounds were fatal, but somehow he pulled through. After his recovery he was promoted to the position of Provost Marshal of the District of Columbia, a position he still held in April 1865 when Lincoln was shot.

At 8.30 pm on 14th April, Abraham Lincoln took his position at Fords Theatre in Washington DC to watch a performance of 'Our American Cousin'. Mr Lincoln sat in the Presidential Box with his wife Mary Todd Lincoln and two guests, Clara Harris and her fiancé Major Henry Rathbone.

At 10.13 pm, Southern sympathiser John Wilkes Booth stepped into the box behind the presidential party. Levelling a derringer pistol at the back of Abraham Lincoln's head, he pulled the trigger. The bullet penetrated Lincoln's brain, mortally wounding him. Major Rathbone reacted first, lunging at the assassin, but Booth stabbed him in the arm. Booth made his escape by leaping onto the stage, fracturing his ankle in the process.

He reputedly roared out 'Sic simper tyrannis' (Thus always to tyrants) before making his escape.

For major James Rowan O'Beirne, it was the start of a night he would never forget.

After John Wilkes Booth's attack, the dying President of the United States was carried from Fords Theatre across the road to William Peterson's Boarding House, where he was carefully placed in one of the rooms. As the Provost Marshal, James O'Beirne was in charge of Lincoln's deathbed and those who had access to the room.

He later recorded the experience:

I was officially present as Provost Marshal of the District of Columbia, but with short intervals of absence, too insignificant to be unaware of any important event which transpired in the room where the great Lincoln lay on his deathbed. From the time when he was first carried into the modest guesthouse, I was at or near Secretary Stanton's side, under his orders most of the time, and stood near him in the gray of the morning when Mr Lincoln died. When first brought through he was more than comatose, hardly breathing. At the suggestion of the physician, a civilian then in charge of him ran to the restaurant next door to the theater and procured a large sarsaparilla glass of Brandy, this was poured down Mr Lincoln's throat and seemed to re-establish respiration.

O'Beirne recalled how Mary Todd Lincoln, utterly grief stricken, knelt at the bedside and bowed her head towards the President's face. Despite the shock of the event the Provost Marshal had to remain mindful of his duty. When it became apparent that Lincoln would die, Secretary of War Edwin Stanton asked O'Beirne to travel to the Kirkwood House Hotel in the city and bring Vice-President Andrew

Johnson to the scene. James O'Beirne was fortunate that there was anyone there to collect. Incredibly, Booth's shooting of Abraham Lincoln had only been part of a wider plot that had been put into operation on 14th April. Secretary of State, William Seward had been attacked in his home and had been stabbed by another accomplice, Lewis Powell, but Seward managed to survive.

Meanwhile, George Atzerodt had been given the task of murdering the Vice-President, and had rented a room above his target in the Kirkwood House for that purpose. However, he lost his nerve and fled before he could carry out the act.

Having secured Vice-President Johnson, Major O'Beirne returned to the Peterson boarding house and brought him to see Lincoln. Afterwards Stanton and Johnson had a discussion in the front room, and the Secretary of War began to dictate messages to foreign governments, informing them of the assassination. It was now the morning of the 15th April and Lincoln's end was near. O'Beirne was present when the President died, and the moment became seared in his memory.

> *When Mr Lincoln breathed his last in a guttural, gasping struggle for breath, Mr Stanton was looking out of the window into the breaking twilight of morning dawn, with one foot on a chair, and holding its back with his right hand, as he leaned with his left elbow on his bended knee.*

The time was 7.22am. As Provost Marshal, James O'Beirne was responsible for organising a manhunt to find the Lincoln conspirators. He first decided to return to the Kirkwood House, where he discovered the room of George Atzerodt, the man who was to have killed Vice-President Johnson. In searching the room he discovered a revolver and ammunition, a bowie knife, a handkerchief belonging to David Herold (he had guided Lewis Powell to Secretary Seward's house) and a bank book belonging to John Wilkes Booth. The key find though was a map of lower Maryland – the neighbouring state to Washington D.C. The hunt was on!

On Sunday 16th April Secretary of War Stanton issued an order to O'Beirne:

> *Major O'Beirne, you are relieved from all other duty at this time and directed to employ yourself and your detective force in the detection*

and arrest of the murderers of the president and the assassins who attempted to murder Mr Seward and make report from time to time.

The Lincoln conspirators had split up. John Wilkes Booth and one of his accomplices, David Herold, escaped Washington altogether, and as the map found in Atzerodt's room suggested they had fled into Maryland.

James O'Beirne's men were hot on their heels. Members of his team went to the Surratt Tavern in Surratsville, Maryland, where a John M Lloyd was arrested. After questioning he revealed that Booth and Herold had stopped there on the night of the assassination. The next stop was the house of Dr. Samuel Mudd. O'Beirne suspected he may have been involved, and had jotted in his diary:

Mudd, near Bryanstown. Son of William A Mudd. A wild, rabid man. served more than two years in the rebel army. Is a black hearted man and was possibly a conspirator. See after him.

Booth had indeed called on the doctor, to have the ankle he fractured treated. Mean while, James O'Beirne personally led eight detectives to Port Tobacco, Maryland, where they arrived on 18th April. The discovered that conspirator David Herold had been there three weeks before and had told friends he would be leaving the country. O'Beirne also questioned a widow who admitted she was in love with George Atzerodt, who had been in town just before the assassination.

Now unsure as to whether Booth had fled to the Maryland swamps or had crossed the Potomac into Virginia, it was decided that O'Beirne and his men would continue to scour Maryland, while the Chief of the National Detective Police, Lafayette C Baker, would concentrate on the Virginia side of the river.

On the 26th April 1865 John Wilkes Booth and David Herold were surrounded in a barn on the Garrett Farm, Virginia, by Lafayette Baker and a detachment of men from the 16th New York Cavalry. The horse soldiers were led by Lieutenant Edward P Doherty, who had been born in Canada to County Sligo parents. The confrontation that ensued led to Herold's capture and the mortal wounding of John Wilkes Booth.

All the central characters had now been hunted down. The man who stabbed Secretary Seward, Lewis Powell, had been captured in Washington on the 17th April, while the Vice-President's would-be assassin, George Atzerodt was arrested in Maryland on the 20th of the month. They would now pay the ultimate price for their crimes. On 7th July 1865, Herold, Powell and Atzerodt were hanged along with Mary Surratt who had owned the boarding house where the conspirators had met before the assassination.

James Rowan O'Beirne.

James Rowan O'Beirne had not been there when John Wilkes Booth had finally been tracked down. Having led the chase for so long, it must have been difficult for the Major not to have witnessed the final moment of drama. Although Baker had taken the ultimate glory of Booth's capture, Secretary of War Stanton was well aware of the key part O'Beirne had played in the manhunt:

> *"You have done your duty nobly and you have the satisfaction of knowing that if you did not succeed in capturing Booth, it was, at all events, certainly the information which you gave that led to it."*

The Provost Marshal received a small portion of the reward money that had been offered for the capture of those involved in killing Lincoln.

He was also breveted (given the Honorary Rank of, but without pay or authority) a Brigadier General of Volunteers for gallant and meritorious services on 26th Sept 1865.

CHAPTER

15

MILLS

Many of our younger readers might be surprised to learn that the town had two active mills at one time. That there was a Windmill at Knock will come as no surprise, but that there was a Water Mill at Barnacor might.

KNOCK WINDMILL

It is not known when the windmill at Knock was first built but records of the area suggest there was one from at least the 1720s. A history of windmill construction suggests that mills built in the early part of the 18th century were cylindrical in shape, while those built from about the 1780s onwards tended to be larger and tapered towards the top. The windmill at Knock, because of its size and cylindrical shape, compares with mills built in the earlier period.

No specific reference can be found as to the mills exact function, but its size and shape suggests that it was almost certainly a corn mill, probably used to grind oats.

Almost nothing is known of the exact details of the mills workings, but from study of similar structures like the windmill at Elphin, a certain configuration can be speculated on. One can reasonably assume that, from the restricted space within the tower, only one set of millstones were in operation here. These millstones would have been situated on the first floor, allowing ground meal to be channeled to the ground floor for bagging.

The roof or cap, would almost certainly have been thatched and would have been the first thing to deteriorate once the mill no longer functioned as such.

The sails, would have been a wooden lattice over which canvas was spread in order to catch the wind. Again, from studies elsewhere it can be assumed that Knock had four sails. Sail size is governed by the height of the tower, which at Knock is 23 feet in height. Allowing for a ground clearance of 3 feet, an educated guess would put the sails at about 20 feet long and 4 feet 6 inches wide.

We have very little information regarding Knock windmill but some interesting facts come to light.

On the O/S map of 1837/8 it shows a windmill, however, on earlier maps what is shown is a windmill stump. This gives credence to the story that after Knock ceased as a conventional corn grinding windmill it may well, some time later, have been converted to a weaving mill. Though there is precious little room for looms, such an abundance of power to drive them would have been hard to resist.

According to Lewis's *topographical dictionary:*

"The weaving of linen is carried out in many parts of the parish, (Rathcline) *and great quantities of frieze is also made."*

It is the 'frieze', historians suggest, that was manufactured at the newly remodelled windmill. (Frieze, is a Middle English name for a coarse woollen, plain weave cloth with a nap on one side.) The sort of material a monk's habit might be made from.

BARNACOR MILL or CLYNES MILL

The first mention of a mill at Barnacor is on the 1837 OS map of the area. This map shows both windmill and corn mill.

There is no physical record of flour having actually been milled at Barnacor, but surely it must have been else why build the mill? Also, at the time of *Griffiths Valuation,* John Costello was the occupier of the mill and he was the owner of at least one boat that conveyed flour and cornmeal, via the Shannon to Richmond Harbour and then onwards to Dublin, by canal. *(Griffiths Valuation is a primary resource for historians of the 19th century. This was the first full scale valuation of all property in Ireland and details of these valuations were published between 1847 and 1864.)*

Interestingly, at the time of Griffith's valuation, though John Costello was the occupier, the land and buildings were actually owned by Luke White Jnr.

Luke White Jnr would have been the wealthiest and, probably, most influential person of the time in the Lanesborough area. Not only did he own the property at Barnacor, (listed as, a house, a mill, 45 acres, 3 roods and 32 perches of land) but he also had land in Carrigeens, Lanesborough, Lisrevagh and Tullyvrane.

Luke White Jnr was the son of the Irish bookseller, lottery operator and Whig politician, who in 1798 loaned to the Irish government one million pounds. In 1818 he entered the Houses of Parliament as the member for Leitrim. With the return on his investments he assembled a considerable property portfolio, including Luttrellstown Castle, now a top class luxury resort, hotel and golf complex in Dublin, and also some in Park Street Mayfair, where he died in 1824.

He left properties worth £175,000 per annum. (According to the U.K. Inflation Calculator, this would be worth 22 million pounds today.)

Luke White Jnr lived in Rathcline House, one of eight children. His brother Samuel represented Leitrim like his father, while Luke Jnr was the MP for Longford. His brother Henry was ennobled to the Peerage of the UK as Baron Annaly of Rathcline. Luke White Jnr died in 1854.

When a valuation review was carried out in 1863–'64, Thomas Clyne was now the occupier of Barnacor Mill and George Walpole the lessor.

What the Water Wheel may well have looked like.

In 1888 a kiln and store had been added to the list of buildings and Patrick A Clyne was now the occupier. From the 1890s to 1931 Teresa Clyne occupied the premises at which time Patrick A Clyne's name reappears, now surely an elderly man.

By the mid-1950s the developing of the bogs by Bord na Móna had so reduced the water levels of Lough Bannow that the flow of water to the mill was now insufficient to operate the mill wheel.

CHAPTER

16

RATHCLINE CASTLE

Rathcline castle is an important monument, situated as it is beside a reed-filled shallow bay, which must once have given access to Lough Ree.

Today, it consists of the dilapidated remnants of a late medieval tower house, an attached 17th century mansion, a substantial Bawn (a defensive wall surrounding a tower house) and a garden site.

The original castle was built and occupied by the Faghny O'Farrells in the 16th century. For a time it may have been held by their vassals, the O'Quinns. In the 1620s, as part of the shake up associated with the Longford Plantation, Rathcline with 2000 acres passed to the English settler, Sir Thomas Dutton, who took up residence bringing with him 2 bulls, 30 cows, 300 ewes, 20 rams, 2 horses and 10 mares. Irish rebels expelled the Duttons from Rathcline during the upheavals of the 1640s.

The property was subsequently acquired by Sir George Lane (1620–'83), a Roscommon man with an O'Farrell grandmother. Sophisticated and well travelled, Lane was secretary to the all powerful Duke of Ormond and was a considerable figure in the Restoration in Ireland, becoming 1st Viscount Lanesborough in 1674.

Surviving 17th century family papers that include a plan and inventory to Rathcline, considerably add to our knowledge of the castle in its heyday.

In 1682 it was described as 'a very noble and spacious house, the seat being very pleasant and well improved with orchards, gardens, fishponds and a deer park. Lane actually planned a replacement house on the site but this was never built.

The castle was destroyed during the war of the kings, The Williamite war, (1688–'91) and seems never to have been re-occupied.

The tower house, representing the era of O'Farrell / O'Quinn has only its east wall extant. Square in plan with a sharp Batter on its lower courses. (A Batter is a receding slope of a wall, structure or earthwork.) It now extends to only three storeys, but would have originally been much higher. The principle room or hall would have been situated on the uppermost floor and the tower possibly topped with crenellated battlements. Its function, in common with that of hundreds of such towers dating from late-medieval Ireland, was to provide a fortified, vertical living space for an elite family in troubled and insecure times.

The 17th century manor house adjoining the tower to the north allowed the inhabitants to enjoy a more spacious horizontal living space. It is likely that the original house was the work of the Duttons in the 1630s. Enough survives to the east and north faces to show that it consisted of at least three story's, with a line of different floors suggested by external stringcourses (a raised horizontal course of bricks). A large flat mullioned window on the first floor is indicative of the original fenestration. The fact that this window has been blocked up is indicative that it, (and possibly others) were replaced by taller wooden frame windows, now visible on either side, probably in the course of improvements made by Sir George Lane.

The London Gazette – May 1681:

Dublin may 2nd.
The Right Honorable George Lord Viscount Lanesborough for the Encouragement of Protestants to dwell and inhabit in the Corporation of Lanesborough in the county of Longford in the Kingdom of Ireland; has declared under his hand, that such of them as will come and dwell in the said Corporation, and build houses, and improve there, shall have Leases for one and twenty years, or for three Lives, Rent-free for the first seven years, and for the remaining years or time, they shall pay such moderate rents as shall be agreed upon, according to the quality of their Holdings wherein they may not doubt of good Encouragement.

The large windows indicate that the first floor contained the principle residential rooms of the house. The second floor windows were probably dormers. A west wing, no longer extant, contained the main door and stairs. The interior walls were probably wooden. An inventory of 1688 refers to the 'damask room', 'dining room', 'old drawing room', and 'my lords dressing room. The windows on the east side probably lit the 'great chamber' which was the principle room of the house for dining and social interaction. Nurseries and servants 'garrets' are also mentioned. Paintings in the castle collection included portraits of the Stuart kings, the Duke of Ormond and his sons, and other members of the aristocracy and gentry to whom the Lanes were connected.

A second arched gateway to the west of the Bawn gateway, has medieval decoration. A third gateway accessed the walled garden to the east. A walkway ran along the interior of the crenellated perimeter wall which was guarded at each corner by flanking towers with musket loops. These towers also provided extra accommodation as shown by the fire places in the south-east tower.

Nothing remains of other ancillary buildings that would have been in the grounds, a bakehouse, a brew house, a slaughterhouse and a porters lodge, all are gone. The only surviving remnants are those of a 19th century farmhouse and other farm buildings.

First published by the County Longford Historical Society.

CHAPTER

17

THE BRIDGE

The River Shannon is the greatest in these islands.

It rises in the north of County Cavan in the Culceagh Mountains from a small pool known as the Shannon Pot. About 8 metres in diameter, this pool is fed by many underground streams running off the mountains. (Recent geological surveys have suggested the source can be traced even further north in County Fermanagh.)

Ballyleague Castle.

Beal Átha Liag, the ancient name of Lanesborough says much about the origins of our town. Translated, the name means the 'mouth of the ford of the flagstones'. Here, the River Shannon from the earliest times has had to cross a ridge of limestone rock where it enters Lough Ree, the resultant ford became the first crossing point of the river north of Athlone, and as is common throughout history, settlements grew at such crossing points.

The crossing place played a significant part in the towns early history, in fact it was frequent Viking raids from the 9th to the 11th centuries that brought about the first recorded bridge here.

The Annals of the Four Masters tells us that, 'the causeway of Átha Liag was made by Malachy the second King of Meath', it was part of his strategy to link up with Cathal O'Connor, King of Connaught, in the struggle against the Vikings.

The next bridge was built by Turlough O'Connor, High King of Ireland, to facilitate the movement of his forces east to west. He erected a bridge in the year 1140.

Next arrived the Normans which saw further action at the (now again) ford. In the year 1220, Walter de Lacy crossed into Connaught and attempted to build a castle, the remains of which can still be seen in Ballyleague. In 1228, the Normans built a castle on the east bank, to maintain control of the ford, known as Meares Fort, this stood where the car park is now, behind St Mary's Hall.

In 1651, following the success of Cromwell's offensive, remnants of Owen Roe's army found themselves in Ballyleague (as the whole town was then known) under the command of General Richard O'Farrell, again they came under attack from the advancing English forces, they were forced to surrender and evacuate Meares Fort and retreat west.

One of the terms of surrender was that: (As recorded in Canon Hurley's notes.) (Captain O'Farrell)

> *'Shall be received into protection and live in the island of Lough Bannow, and have the liberty of twelve musketeers to defend himself and familie from idle persons provided he gives security that they shall not act anything prejudicial to the state of England.'*

After the Battle of the Boyne in 1690, Sarsfield (Patrick Sarsfield, 1st Earl of Lucan) withdrew westward to defend the line of the Shannon. Colonel Edmund O'Reilly, a native of Cavan was in charge of the defences. In December, the Williamite army under General Kirk, approached with a view of breaking through across the ford. O'Reilly withdrew to the west bank and destroyed the flimsy wooden bridge that had been erected near the ford. The Williamites took up their positions on the east bank and the two armies spent the winter of 1690-91 watching each other across the river. The war eventually ended but the bridge was not repaired, people now had to wade across as before or take a ferry if the water was high. On the morning of Fair Day in 1702, the ferry was crowded with people all carrying their goods and products to sell at the fair. We don't know what the weather was like on this cold February morning, or whether it was a factor or not, but the ferry capsized and 35 of the 46 souls on board perished in the Shannon depths.

As a result of this terrible accident, Parliament was petitioned to have a new bridge built across the river and, four years later in 1706, the first stone bridge at Lanesborough was completed. The stones used for the building were those from the now dismantled Meares Fort. It was however, a Toll Bridge, and those unwilling or unable to pay the new tolls, walked 50 metres downstream and took their chances wading across as they had previously done. According to Isaac Weld, the bridge, built in 1706 consisted of nine arches, at the centre of which was an inscription bearing this date carved below the coat of arms of the Lane family with the following inscription:

The Arms of the right hon. Lord Viscount Lanesborough who gave £100 towards the construction of this bridge.

We have the Toll Charges for 1717 and they were as follows:
Every man or woman. 1 penny.
One horse or one cow. 1 penny.
Six sheep, pigs or goats. 1 penny.
One barrel of grain. 1/2 penny.

Today we have the distillery producing fine spirit products but, in the early 19th century, on the east bank, in perhaps a similar position to the distillery was a brewery. The beer brewed here had a good reputation, and it was said that it was flavoured with bog berries, which grew abundantly in the neighbouring bogs.

A pint of Bog-Berry Bitter, alliterative ale, no less.

By the early 19th century the industrial revolution was in full swing in the UK and many improvements had been made in agriculture as well.

The population of Ireland in 1841 was estimated at 8.18 million people, higher than it has ever been at any time, within fifty years it would be barely half that number (at the 2022 census the population of Ireland was recorded at 5,149,139).

This rising population needed to be fed and clothed but the infrastructure in Ireland was very poor. The road network was in places awful and susceptible to the elements, Isaac Weld described the 'day coach' travelling the road between Roscommon and Longford:

> *"...up drove the day coach, dashing and splashing, falling and floundering, and at last crawling out of this slough of despond and moving mass of mud, devoid of shape or form baffling description."*

The above just goes to show the importance of the Shannon in moving goods around. There had been some foresight in the need of a better infrastructure resulting in the Grand Canal being completed in 1804 and the Royal Canal being finished in 1817, however the narrow Shannon at Lanesborough had presented problems.

To help traffic through Lanesborough, it was reported in 1773 that there was a "short canal and one pair of gates with a fall of one foot and five inches at Lanesborough".

The following extract from a letter written by a Lieutenant John Tully R.N. describes the difficulty of getting cargo through Lanesborough:

> *"... We crossed the lake with three boats in tow of the steamer, such a sight was never before witnessed on that lake. On our arrival in Lanesborough our troubles only commenced, which induced me to stay with the boats and see it out. I lighted two of the boats to 2'6" and 2'8" and put their cargo onto the third, being obliged to use some stratagem, not having any boat to spare. the canal is filling up fast, the very walls on its banks are falling into it. We had to take almost the whole cargo out before we could get the boats through."*

This letter of 1831 highlights some of the problems which beset Shannon travellers on the upper reaches of Lough Ree, The levels of Lough Ree vary greatly, but the lowest levels tend to occur on the upper reaches of the lake.

Commissioners for the Navigation of the river Shannon set to work in 1840. They blasted the rock of the old fording place which was an impediment to river traffic, and cut a deep navigation channel along the west bank of the river. This new arrangement to the bridge, with a swivel arch allowing boats with high upper structures to pass through, was opened in 1844. (*See picture, possibly Lord Granard's boat passing through the swing bridge.)*

At about this time *circa 1830*, a survey of the County Roscommon was carried out. It is interesting to note the make-up of our community at about that time:

Lanesborough contains:
67 cabins thatched.
11 cabins without chimneys. 4 new cabins – slated.
11 houses of two stories, slated including a schoolhouse.
5 houses of two stories thatched.
2 houses of three stories, new.

Ballyleague contains:
43 cabins thatched.
5 cabins without chimneys.
2 houses of two stories thatched.
2 new cottages of mortar and stone in progress.
1 Long double cottage, ornamented with garden and flowers in front, neat and pretty.

However, as the twentieth century progressed it was the overhead traffic that threatened the stability of the bridge. By the 1960s the swivel arch had become unstable and a Bailey Bridge was put in place.

The Old Bridge.

The timber planks of the Bailey Bridge rattled so loudly that traffic crossing the river could be heard for miles around. For years the cacophony of the traffic on the bridge became part of the everyday environment.

In the early 1970s, a joint venture between Longford and Roscommon County Councils produced a major overhaul of the bridge. The swivel arch was replaced by a widened and strengthened bridge, needed to cope with the ever increasing volume of road traffic.

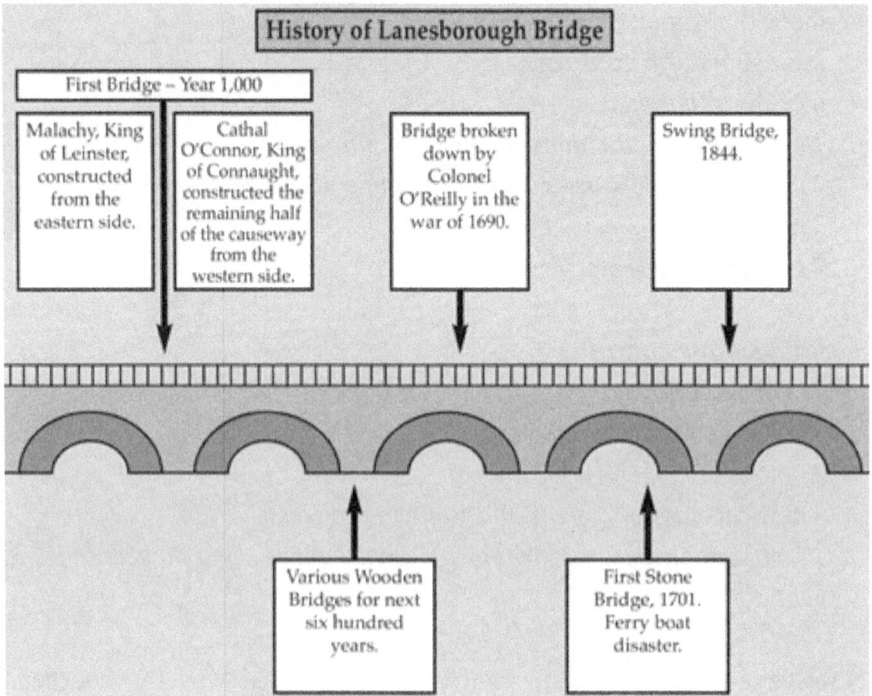

CHAPTER

18

ST. MARY'S CHURCH & ST. JOHN'S CHURCH

Lanesborough

Church of the Holy Rosary – Ballyleague

It is almost 200 years since the community of Lanesborough celebrated its Hatches, Matches and Dispatches from St Mary's Church, Ballymahon Road. Opposite The Green.

First constructed in 1834 on land donated by Luke White, owner of the Rathcline Estate. Not only did he contribute financially to the building of St Mary's, Luke White was regarded as a good landlord who had helped financially and otherwise in the Catholic campaign and the repeal of the penal laws.

The story behind the building of the church is interesting.

The hooves of Luke White's cattle had all been cut off during the night. This had been the custom of the Whiteboys, (*The Whiteboys were a secret Irish Agrarian Society which defended tenant-farmer land rights for subsistence farming. More active in the late 18th century, though there was still a branch operating in the Lanesborough area at this time. They were also known as 'Levellers')* and Luke White concluded that they must have done the misdeed. For this he punished the Catholics severely. After some time however he discovered that it had been in fact Protestants who held a grudge against him who carried out the crime.

Filled with remorse he compensated the Catholics by personally designing a church and providing the finance to build it. There was not a lot of proper supervision on the builders, and they made a mess of the work. Luke White was disgusted and during an argument with the parish priest about the church told him that he himself could build a better cow-shed and refused to pay the money necessary to put a roof on the building. The money was raised by other means and the church completed.

The church has been extensively altered since its first construction in 1834, it was much further developed between this date and 1910.

The old photo of St. Mary's.

A castellated square tower with conical limestone pinnacles on each corner dominates the east end of Lanesborough and is a landmark feature dominating approaching the town from Longford, Ballymahon or Roscommon.

Externally all that remains of the original 19th century ensemble is the dressed stone apse and sacristy to the rear of the church, and limestone window eyebrow hoodmouldings and tower crenellations on the front façade.

In 1958 while Fr. John Quinn was parish priest a major renovation of the church was undertaken including the addition of two wings added to the entrance, therefore, the church standing today is considerably different from that built 190 years ago.

St. John's Church of Ireland

On left is Lanesborough Abbey, now St. John's Church of Ireland.

The above impression was published by Francis Grose in 1792, about a hundred years after the retreating Jacobite army used it for canon target practice from the west bank of the Shannon.

The arch is still standing and is now listed as a national monument.

Going to Church in the days of yore was a very serious matter indeed, Churchgoers at St John's were subject to the following:

CONSTITUTIONS AND CANONS ECCLESIASTICAL 1840

XC. The Duty of Church-wardens touching such Persons as are out of the Church, in time of God's Worship, on Sundays or Holydays.

The Church-wardens and their Assistants shall warn Innholders, Taverners, Victuallers and Alehouse keepers, that they sell no Meat or Drink, and that they receive none into their Tavern or Alehouse, all the Time wherein there is preaching or celebration of Divine Service upon Sundays or Holydays. If any do contrary, upon contempt or stubbornness, they shall present both him and them, whom he received by Name, in the next Visitation. Also they shall see, that none of those light Wanders in Markets, Pelting-sellers, which carry about, and sell Pins, Points, and other small Trifles, whom they call Pedlars, set out their wares to sale: And that no Beggars, or idle persons abide, either in the Church-yard, or near the Church, all that time, but shall cause them either to come in or depart.

XCI. Their Duty touching those Persons that are in the Church at that time.

They shall also see, that in every meeting of the Congregation, Peace be well kept; and that none behave themselves disorderly in the Church. And to that end, they shall warn the People, that they bring not with them to the Church, Dogs, Hawks with Bells, or Children which are not so nurtured, as if they can be kept quiet in their Seats, without running up and down. Neither shall they suffer any Person to disturb the Service or Sermon, either by untimely Ringing of Bells, or by walking, talking, laughing, or any other Noise which may hinder the Minister, or offend the People. And the names of all such that offend in this kind, shall truly, and personally present in the Ordinates' Visitations.

CHAPTER

19

A FIRM FOUNDATION

If there were no soil, or bog, or grass, or fields, or anything sitting on top of the bedrock that makes Ireland geologically what it is, then you could set off from Monaghan and walk to Mallow in Cork on the same rock. Not only that, you could walk from Dublin to Galway on the same rock.

Laid down between 328–359 million years ago, the rock in question is Lower Carboniferous Limestone, in more familiar terms, it's what the Burren is made from.

Going back not quite so far in history, say, nearly 200 years, and you were walking over the bridge at Lanesborough from the Roscommon side, if you looked to your left towards Kilnacarrow you would encounter a vast wilderness. Look to your right and you would most likely see men working the limestone quarries. At this time these various quarries stretched from Lanesborough Bridge to Newtown Cashel a distance of some 10 kilometres. In terms of employment to the local community, as many people were employed in these quarries as would be employed by Bord na Móna a century later.

So, what is Limestone and what are its main uses.

Limestone is a type of carbonate sedimentary rock, which is the main source of lime.

It has three fundamental uses worldwide. From the very earliest times one of the main uses of limestone has been in architecture. How old? Well the great Pyramid of Giza, built over 2,500 years BC, was built entirely of limestone blocks. How many blocks? — 2.3 million, that is 2,300,000 blocks of limestone - each weighing, on average, 2.6 tonnes - mind boggling!

Perhaps most importantly in Ireland, crushed, powdered limestone is used to re-balance the pH levels of soils. Most agricultural land in Ireland is over acidic, by spreading lime on the fields this balances the pH levels to what they should be, thus providing much healthier growing conditions particularly for grass.

Thirdly, we wouldn't have any concrete or cement without limestone - just imagine how much of that's been used over the years.

There is much evidence of local use of our native limestone. All three of the Lanesborough/ Ballyleague churches were built from it. Other prominent buildings include the three public houses of Lanesborough and, over the bridge, the public house most recently known as Rosies, plus the Sliabh Ban hotel and Shannon View House.

The more recent history of the quarry workings in Lanesborough begins in 1948 when the first of the two quarry workings in Commons North opened to produce lime for agricultural use. Leased from Tom Gill, the quarry was worked under the name of Agricultural Lime Ltd. William Conroy took over the lease in 1952. The first quarry closed sometime in the mid-fifties as its workings grew ever closer to the Rathcline Road.

The old photo of Quarry team.

The second quarry was already underway by this time and continued to operate until circa 1960.

Rock was blasted using gelignite made active with detonators placed in holes drilled close to the top of the rock. In the early years a drill would have been driven in by hand and it would have taken a long time to drill to any depth. These holes would have been 2-inches wide and no deeper than two feet. Later with the introduction of more advanced power drills, sticks of high explosive were placed in 4-inch bore holes to a depth of 20 feet about 10 feet apart. One blasting on this scale would remove enough rock to provide about a weeks' worth of processing.

In the late 1950s the quarry provided employment for approximately 12 people including, a foreman, a clerical officer, a machine maintenance worker, an explosives setter, two salesmen and four drivers.

CHAPTER

20

TALES OF CURREEN

Standing on the bridge at Lanesborough / Ballyleague and facing due south, a broad stretch of the Shannon, as it widens into Lough Ree, is presented to the view. On the Leinster side of the lake stands Curreen Lodge, formerly Salisbury Lodge, as the late Lord Salisbury used the lodge during the summer season of the year.

The Shannon was notoriously difficult to navigate at this particular point so in 1844–'48 the 'Cut', as it is known locally, was engineered.

Previous to this huge improvement to the livelihood of the working boats of the river, it had to be dredged every few years. The dredged portion was semi-circular in shape and approx 100–150 metres in length.

On each excavation, fresh and exciting debris would be dragged ashore. These items would range from domestic utensils of all kinds to many,

many old implements of warfare spanning the years.

Rude swords, cuirasses, round stones, lumps of lead and even old barrels of salted meat *(a cuirass was body armour, usually a breastplate and backplate joined together. A mounted soldier wearing such equipment became known as cuirassier).*

It would be a regular activity for the children of the area to scour and search the riverbank for such treasure after any dredging work had taken place. It begs the question, why was all this treasure in the one place?

Well, one answer may be the fact that in 1690 there was no bridge at Lanesborough, and the Williamite troops who were in retreat from their defeat in Athlone, decided that here they would attempt to cross the river. A floating bridge of logs and small boats was cobbled together, but when the actual crossing was attempted, the Williamite infantry were attacked by the local Irish and driven back into the woods of Rathcline.

Some days following this first engagement, the attack was renewed, this time covered by cavalry, a very blood-thirsty conflict ensued in which many a rider and horse, friend and foe, found a final resting place at the curve of the Shannon at Curreen.

Researched by John Casey – from Longford Library.

ACCESS FOR ALL centre.

Many thanks to the superb ACCESS FOR ALL team for their help with the above photographs.

CHAPTER

21

THE SCHOOL IN THE FIELD

by: John Casey

My memory drifts back to the 1950s, when Lanesborough was then embarking on what might be described as its own Celtic Tiger. Many new big ventures were opening up which would change the local landscape as well as the area's prospects.

The introduction of Bord na Móna, a lime producing factory and the first ESB generating station, which was started in 1955 and became operational in 1958. All these revolutionary developments led to an inward migration of workers from all four corners of Ireland. This in turn led to new housing being built on The Green, in Cloontuskert and Derryhaun. Many of the incoming families grew and blended into the community, so much so that the younger generation of today is unlikely to be aware of the diverse and varied backgrounds of their friends and neighbours.

At the same time as these industrial advances, but no less significant, came the Girls' National School (Scoil Mhuire Gan Smál) which was officially opened in May 1959 by Patrick Hillery, who was the Minister for Education at the time. Also in attendance to bless this fine building were: the Bishop, James McNamee, Canon William Quinn PP Rathcline, Fr. Lawrence O'Grady CC Rathcline, Canon John Wall, administrator Longford Cathedral and a large contingent of TDs and Councillors.

The site for the new school was purchased from Tommy Gill who lived on the Rathcline Road. Tommy also supplied the site for the new generating station that would make electricity from turf. The local population was fascinated by it all. Naturally, a new road was constructed for the school and the new ESB station – before this it was known as Church Lane which extended as far as Aughamore, a summer farm owned by Paddy Farrell.

The contractors for the new school were McLoughlins of Longford, who were well-known builders of schools and churches at that time. Gill's field, as it was known, was flanked on one side by the Church of Ireland and the town's gardens which consisted of Gallaghers, Caseys, Moores, Greenes, Miss Dolans, Farrells, the Lough Ree Arms (McNallys), McGuinness, the Northern Bank and the Shannon side by McRann's orchard, latterly the Convent of the Sisters of Mercy.

It's hard to believe now but in the late 1940s and early 1950s there were 75 children living on the Main Street, from the church to the bridge. In those days, with no radio or television we had to make our own entertainment. Gill's field was one of the many places where we re-enacted the magical films we had seen in Eddie Kelly's cinema in Tullyvrane, films such as, *Billy The Kid, The James Gang, Hop-Along Cassidy* and many more. Tommy Gill didn't seem to mind when he came to bring his cows home for milking of an evening.

Another major recreational event for us children was the bringing home of the hay from Gill's field. Many a happy harvest evening was spent 'helping' Paddy McGuinness – Tommy Gill's farm worker – bringing in the hay on the shifter. Of course we were more of a hindrance than a help, but Paddy knew we loved the 'drosie' on the shifter.

The Church Lane would be a hive of activity on a Sunday afternoon when the young men from the parish would take part in a game of Pitch & Toss. Of course we had to be very vigilant to stay out of view of the Guards and even more especially out of view of the local curate. These leaders of Church and State left us in no doubt as to what would happen if we carried on this immoral and irreverent practice of gambling.

I recall Gill's field underwent its own changes during the Second World War, and for some years afterwards. The Government brought in a scheme called the Compulsory Tillage Act. Every farmer had to plant a percentage of his land in corn. Gill's field came under the Act, and I can remember the men harvesting that lovely golden corn with a reaper and binder which would have been new at the time.

If I mention 'Paugheen's Well', I wonder how many people would know what or where I was talking about. Paugheen's Well was on the perimeter of the two sites of the school and generating station. It was one of the town's three wells along with Whisky Well, now the Duck Pond, and Father O'Flynn's well.

Of the three, in my youth Paugheen's Well was much the better known and I remember its distinct cool freshness.

CHAPTER

22

INCHCLEURAN IN LOUGH REE

Some years ago the well known local historian Seán Cahill wrote a short history of Inis Clothrann and we have pleasure here in reproducing the chapter entitled MYTH AND LEGEND.

Some eighty acres of green sward rise from the waters of Lough Ree, lying almost directly north - south and dividing this expanse of water equidistant from the Longford and Roscommon shores. Tradition, legend and mythology ascribe to this place an enchanting and colourful past reaching far into the ages of pre-history.

Inis Clothrann is the island of Clothra, the legendary sister of the famous Queen Maeve of Connaught, and there are many references to it in the Táin Bó Culainge and contemporary literature. Earthworks, placenames on the island and the oral tradition of an island-people are still the evidence to authenticate the island's claim to fame at the dawn of our history. Centuries later saw the emergence of one of our earliest Christian monasteries which flourished for a thousand years and survives today, only in the ruined cloisters and desecrated altars whose mute stories attest to the glory that once was the holy place. Since the sacking of the monastic buildings and the confiscation of lands almost five centuries ago by King Henry VIII of England, the island has experienced varied fortunes including decay and plunder. The lands have seen many owners and suffered many changes until today, when the island lies uninhabited, sleeping peacefully in the quiet solitude of Lough Ree.

The story of Inis Clothrann falls naturally into three sections. The first section will deal with the prehistoric legendary story of the island. The second, which ranges from the sixth to sixteenth century, will cover the monastic period. The third section covers the period from the sixteenth century, which may be described as the later or modern story of the island.

As has already been stated, the name of the island is derived from Clothra, sister of Maedhbh, the warrior queen, who is reputed to have lived about a century before Christ. No scrap of legend or tradition regarding Clothra has survived. Her fame rests entirely on having been Maedhbh's sister and on having left her name to the island. Tradition associates the name of Maedhbh with at least three key locations. On the centre of the island, which is incidentally its highest point of elevation above sea-level, there are earthworks and the remains of a ring-fort which were traditionally described as Dún Maedhbha. The great antiquarian and scholar, John O'Donovan reports his visit to the island in 1837.

He recounts his conversations with one James Moran, whom he describes as the oldest inhabitant of the island at this time. James Moran, as a child in the 1750s remembered the walls of the Dun still standing and stated that the stones were carried away to build a rough ditch which divided the island into two properties and may be seen to this day.

It is of significance that later generations continued to associate these very stones to the famous queen. Evidence of this can be found in a delightful article written by Mary Banim about 1889, and published in her book, *'Here And There In Ireland'* in 1891. Miss Banim repeats verbatim what she heard from old Dan Farrell and from his wife who was then 85 years. Mrs. Farrell recounted the tale of a drowning accident and the banshee who she heard keening and whose crying led the man to the discovery of the body that had just been washed ashore. Mary Banim concludes ... 'It is certain that no one who lives on Inis Clothrann has ever doubted that it was the banshee whose wail was heard as she issued from the old home of Queen Maedhbh and treaded her way along the shore, from the Grianan down to the lake … .'

The Grianan mentioned here is the next significant place related to the queen. Today, it is overgrown with shrubbery and bushes and can only be approached with difficulty. Located a short distance to the east of the Dun it would appear to have been quite visible and accessible to O'Donovan. He was shown it by the inhabitants who called it Grianan Meva. Some 250 metres to the east of the Grianan we come to an astonishing landmark. A small knoll or cairn in the field known as Beor-Laighionn is surmounted by a thorn bush. O'Donovan was taken to this spot which was pointed out to him as Inidmarfameva, and in precisely this form he had it marked on the ordnance survey map. We heard from the islanders the famous legend of the death of Maedhbh which forms part of the old story of the Táin. This story can also be found in Ceitinn's *'Foras Feasa'* Vol. II. It was a revenge killing having its roots in the 'Táin Wars'. Forbuidh, son of Conchuir Mac Nessa, King of Ulster, had a score to settle and he killed queen Maedhbh, 'with a lic of a stone' hurled from Elfeet Bay, more than a mile distant on the eastern shore.

This is regarded by some scholars as the final and concluding event of the Táin Bó Culainge. Whatever one may think about the accuracy or otherwise of the detail, there is no doubt whatever that the well-knit community of a tiny island people preserved this lore both in the oral tradition and in the place-names and handed it on from generation to generation down through the ages.

The 18th century artist Daniel Grosse (1766-1838)
painted two pictures on a visit to the island,
these are pictured opposite.

The site of a 6th century monastery.

The ruins of Clogas Church.

It's hard to imagine a community from the 6th century - even harder to imagine that that community had been in existence over 400 years, when, in 988 Brian Boru sailed his ever-growing fleet north into Lough Ree to make battle with the Conatians.

The battle at Lough Ree was a resounding victory for Brian in that Muirgheas the tánaiste of Connacht was killed, as was Dhúnlaing, tánaiste of Desmond.

Subsequently, Brian Boru is regarded as the man who drove the Vikings out of Ireland and became its first unifying king. He died at Clontarf in 1014.

CHAPTER

23

THE RATHCLINE MAN-TRAP

In 1821, Luke White Jnr built Rathcline House, from where, for the greater part of the 19th century, the White family were the major landlords of Lanesborough town and Rathcline parish.

In 1860, some six years after Luke's death, the White family left Rathcline and leased the demesne to a Mr. George Johnston, locally known, somewhat unkindly, as 'Stick Foot' Johnston because he had a wooden leg.

Despite his impediment, Mr. Johnston managed to farm the land for the best part of forty years until his death in the late 1890s. At his death, the lands were sold to the sitting tenants through the Irish Land Commission. The house and home farm were sold to the Geoffrey family, who farmed it for another 50 plus years.

In 1954 the house was sold to The Sisters of Mercy, but prior to this sale there was an auction of household furniture and farm machinery.

Mr. Cecil English, who resides near Athlone, told me he attended the auction and purchased a box of small farmyard implements, when he arrived home and examined the contents, to his amazement, he discovered that one of the items was a 'man-trap' in perfect condition.

Chambers Encyclopedia (1908) described a man-trap thus:

Engines for the terrifying of trespassers and poachers (formerly often indicated by the warning notice 'man-traps and spring guns set here').

Resembling giant rat-traps as much as four feet long.

They may be seen in museums - the man-trap in question was on display in Athlone museum - but since 1827 it has been illegal to set them outside. It was for some time legal to set them inside the home between sunset and sunrise as a defence against burglars.

Michael Corcoran told me that his father worked on the Rathcline estate at the end of the 19th century and in his opinion the man-trap was never set inside or outside the house.

This fearsome piece of equipment can be seen in the excellent Athlone Castle Museum.

CHAPTER

24

EVICTION STONE (1814)

Moneen is a townland about four miles from Lanesborough on the Roscommon side of the Shannon river, and in the parish of Kilgefin. Here in the boundary wall of an old schoolhouse, is a very unique stone carving.

The carving depicts an eviction scene, and the layout is as follows: A small farmhouse with a cat to one side and a dog to the other; what appears to be a soldier on the right hand side; and another figure to the left. Underneath a date of 1814 is inscribed.

For the duration of World War II and beyond, Roscommon County Council demolished quite a number of old buildings, stones from which were used to both build new and repair existing roads. The story goes that the house of one Peter Davis, who lived in the townland of Antrabeg, about three miles from Lanesborough, was demolished in the year 1943. The name Spollen is said to have been associated with the stone. It is my opinion that Spollen may have been the sculptor, though no one knows for sure.

According to tradition, the sheriff and the military arrived to carry out an eviction and that, according to the law, all animals and humans had to vacate the house before the eviction could proceed. However, each time they charged the house, the cat and dog appeared inside. This was considered a sinister omen and in time the military withdrew. It would seem the eviction never took place. It is most likely that this stone was carved to commemorate the failure of the eviction.

As far as I know, there is no record of any similar stone to be found in Ireland. When the old house eventually came to be demolished, the stone was removed and relocated to its present position by the then school teacher Miss Fox.

The author and editor visited the site in February 2024. the stone is still visible, but was so overgrown it was impossible to take a new photograph.

CHAPTER

25

IMPORTANT VISITORS TO LANESBOROUGH

Imagine the scene – the year is 1885, August, and to our little community come two of the biggest political figures of the time.

Imagine further what a sight to that small community it must have been, as the party approached Lanesborough from Longford station – 150 horseman parading in front of 40 local bands from the surrounding parishes, the pageantry of which had never been seen before or since.

Who were our illustrious visitors? They were John Redmond and Michael Davitt.

John Redmond was an Irish Parliamentary MP who later led the party following the death of Charles Stewart Parnell in October 1891, and who is remembered as a statesman who made a vital contribution to the creation of the Irish State. At the time he came to the Lanesborough meeting he was the Member of Parliament for New Ross.

The Irish National Land League was founded at the Imperial Hotel Castlebar in October 1879. At the inaugural meeting Parnell was voted in as the first Chairman and Michael Davitt as one of the Honorary Secretaries.

Such was the feeling for land reform that many 'monster meetings' were held all over Ireland. The first of these was held in Irishtown near Claremorris on 20th April 1879 which had an estimated turnout of 15–

20,000 people. One can only assume that it was such a strength of feeling that this demonstrates which led to the founding of the Land League the following year.

Michael Davitt, as well as being a founding member of the Land League was also an early organiser within the Irish Republican Brotherhood. In 1870 he was convicted and sentenced to seven years in prison for arms trafficking.

On his release from prison Davitt pioneered the New Departure strategy which aimed to unite the 'physical force' and 'constitutional' wings of Irish Nationalism. The Land League sought to resolve the issue of absentee landlordism and bring relief to the tenant farmers by securing fixity of tenure, fair rent and free sale of the tenant's interest.

We know a little of the speeches that were made – the RIC transcribed Davitt's words.

Speaker M Davitt:

"When gazing today with pride upon hundreds of Land League cavalry, and looking down from this platform upon the thousands of manly faces, my thoughts travel back two hundred years in the history of Ireland, when Sarsfield (First Earl of Lucan and a leading figure in Jacobite army during the Williamite war in Ireland) *and his gallant followers dashed by the side of the lordly Shannon to give battle to the foe (cheers); but though we are not here today with lances couched and swords in hand to fight for Irelands rights, still we are here with hearts as brave and purpose as strong as when other weapons than those of ours were used on behalf of Ireland. Just as the valour of Sarsfield and his men hurled back the enemy from the walls of Athlone, so has the strength of Irish national sentiment hurled the representatives of the government from this platform today."*

Speaker Redmond was even a little more bellicose. His words reported as follows:

Speaker Redmond:

Said he had been introduced to the meeting by their respected priest as one of the rebel Irish Party *(cheers)*. That statement he accepted as a compliment, and that statement is simply the truth, because we are today rebelling against English rule *(cheers)* as ever Patrick Sarsfield was when he treaded this land and fought for its liberties. If we are without weapons in our hands, we have at least, thank God, the same spirit, the same deadly hatred for England *(cheers)*. And if poor Sarsfield, when he was pouring out his hearts blood for a foreign cause upon a foreign soil, could have looked far into the future and see the spirit which animates you today, he would die still more happily in the knowledge that the cause for which he fought, was the cause that will be continued to be fought for by the Irish race, as long as any flag is in this country but our own. *(cheers)*

We are here to declare to our brethren of the universal world that we will not cease working for Ireland until Ireland is as she once was, on an equal footing with the nations of the world.

Speaker Redmond denounced Landlordism as:

> *"Landlords were simply, before god, the greatest and most successful robbers that the world ever knew".*

The *Irish Times* on the 22/08/1885 reported the event as follows:

> *"On Sunday a demonstration was held at Lanesborough, seven miles from Longford. contingents arrived from parts of Roscommon, Longford and surrounding districts. over thirty branches of the National League were represented. A large contingent escorted Messrs. Davitt and Redmond from Longford to the place of the meeting and were met half way by about 150 horsemen bearing national emblems, who acted as a guard of honour. At a late hour the chair was taken by Rev. Father McGivney, PP of Lanesborough."*

CHAPTER

26

EDWARDIAN MATCHMAKING

What follows are two letters, reprinted in full, that discuss certain events of match- making that took place in the first decade of the 20th century.

The only thing that has changed is ALL the names. The real names involved are still prominent in the local area and we have no wish to cause embarrassment to anybody. *(Ed)*

Dear Patrick

In reply to your welcome letter of the 22 instant which leaves us all very happy to know that you are improving, thanks to God, I know you will be sorry to hear that Billy Smith is coming home to be interred on this day. It is poor news for his poor mother that reared him so nice.

Well, I want to tell you about some business we have in hand at the present. Jim Stone is setting a match for Audrey this last week with Walter Byrne in Lanesboro, that is Kath Mulryan's son. I don't know do you know him. He has a good place and well stocked. It was himself first introduced it but he wanted too much money. He asked for £200 and said he had had it to get in three places but that his mother told him to try here first. Well I was very near believing him for I know the places. One of them is Killooly, Mary McMahon in Moher is her aunt and John Murphy and Mary McMahon is a long time trying to bring him there.

We told Jim Stone to tell him that we would give him £150 and he did not agree but he came again to Jim Stone and told him that his mother persevered on him and he is to come to our house on next Wednesday night himself and Jim Stone and the last shilling we have is £105. I don't know if I am putting the figures right or not but they mean one hundred and fifty.

Audrey went through her money too fast and I couldn't stop her when she would go to Mass and have all the cares passing her by she would be wild when she would come home so the cart and harness and cane and harness cost too much.

This fellow is living now for himself in Billy's old houses but has them well fixed. old Billy owned half of that place and his father owned the other half and he has all now. We would like it well if we could get through it. We are just able to leave down the hundred and fifty but that is as I said before the last shilling.

I will conclude by hoping this finds you in good health. Let me know what you think about this subject.

From your auld father
Fergus, Lanesboro Co. Longford.

These are not the easiest letters to read, but we have published them as they were written.

A few days later Fergus wrote to Patrick Gain:

Dear Patrick.

In reply to your welcome letter of this morning, happy to hear that your hopes is good, thanks be to God. I would like to have a letter every day from you if possible. Well dear Patrick we had Walter Byrne and Jim Stone here last night. We settled with him very nicely. We counted him out a hundred and fifty pounds and he felt satisfied. We didn't even get into bargaining with him for I very well knew he knew where to go. He was even invited out to Fermoyle to Shay Toms. The marriage day is not fixed yet but I think it will be about this day week. Walter Byrne is a bit dragged with the world and a little old but there is not any nonsense about Audrey and she says herself is not very young. I have no need to say much for I see you know as much about the case yourself as I do.

I am writing a few lines to Kenneth and Sam to see if they could come home for a day or two and to send me a little help for this time to make a wedding. That is all we are short. It will not take a lot. Fowl is plenty.

From you auld father
Fergus

CHAPTER

27

NEWTOWNCASHEL

Population Exodus

In the year 1841 the population of Ireland stood at 8.18 million, greater than it has ever been before or since. In the same year, 1841 the parish of Newtowncashel recorded a population of 5,461. This figure illustrates just how densely populated a typical rural Irish parish was at the time.

As a result of the ravages of famine and emigration and the continued failure of the potato crop in successive years, by 1851 the parishes population had decreased by 34% to 3,563. This started a cycle of rural depopulation which has continued to this day, By the year 1983 Newtowncashel parish recorded a population of 999, barely 18% of the pre-famine total.

There are a number of reasons for this rural exodus, financial and social among others. In the aftermath of The Great Hunger both landlord and tenant displayed a marked reluctance for total reliance on the potato as a source of nutrition. The landlords incurred heavy losses during these non-productive years, and the tenants losses were of a much greater degree – they witnessed close family, friends and relatives sicken and die in great numbers. New farming methods and crops were introduced. These new crops required a great deal more acreage to sustain a family. It is estimated that it required six times more ground for corn enough to feed a family compared to the potato. Even after the disaster of the famine the countryside could not support the number of people living there. Emigration was *encouraged* by the masters in the "Big House" and in some cases finance was provided. This was cheaper and less dangerous than the eviction process which left people homeless and dependant on the parish.

The lack of available accommodation, employment and indeed marriage prospects drove many to seek their fortunes in the cities and large towns. Many emigrated to places like Dublin and Liverpool and other cities which were starting to come to terms with growing industrialisation. The new fangled mechanisation increased city based employment and further reduced the need for manual labour and other rural pursuits.

Michael Casey designed monument in Newtown Cashel, carved by Mark Feeley.

CHAPTER

28

LANESBOROUGH / BALLYLEAGUE DIVIDED

In the Spring of 1940, just as the U.K. was about to begin the fight for its existence in The Battle of Britain, matters of a slightly more mundane episode were exercising the good people of Lanesborough / Ballyleague.

The following has been told before, but it's worth re-telling none the less, the piece is taken from an article in the Longford Leader *dated, Saturday April 20th, 1940.*

'Because there is a river and a bridge between them the people will not mix, but sooner that nonsense disappears the better', said District Justice Kenny at Roscommon Court during the hearing of an application for a licence for Maypole dancing in Lanesborough.

Michael Brennan, Secretary of the Ballyleague (Lanesborough) Dance Committee applied for a Maypole dance licence for that locality.

Mr. P.C. Sweeney appeared for the applicant.

Supt. Somers, Roscommon, on behalf of Supt. Dowd, Longford, objected to the application.

Mr. Sweeney said the application was before Mr. McCann, D.J. at the last Court when it was adjourned. The main objection put forward that day was that there was no proper parking space. Since the last Court another agreement had been drawn up with Mr. Gaughran, owner of the field, giving the committee parking space in the field beside the proposed Maypole. He had the Secretary in Court.

Justice: Secretary of what?

Mr. Sweeney: Of the Ballyleague Dance Committee.

The Justice asked what was the object of the committee.

Mr. Sweeney: It is a private concern and they are laying out £100 on it.

Mr. Sweeney added that they had a petition signed by a number of people in and around the village asking to have this Maypole started. There was no amusement in the district.

Michael Brennan, the applicant, produced the original agreement signed by the owner of the field on which they proposed to erect the Maypole. He produced a subsidiary agreement signed since the last Court in connection with the parking facilities.

Witness produced a document signed by a number of people in Ballyleague petitioning for the erection of the Maypole. There was no other suitable site in the locality, except one which was too near the church. They wanted amusement for the people on their side of the bridge.

Justice: Because there is a river and a bridge between them the people will not go across the river. The sooner that nonsense disappears the better, because it is nothing else.

Maypole dancers.

Witness said there was only one dance held every month during the summer in the other dance hall in Lanesborough. These dances would be anything from 2s/6d upwards. The price they proposed to charge at the Maypole was 4d per head.

Supt. Somers said he was objecting on behalf of Supt. Down, Longford, in whose district this Maypole was to be erected. The objections were based on three formal grounds, namely:

1) Unsuitable locality, 2) adequate facilities for dancing already in the area, 3) no parking facilities.

Cross examined by Supt. Somers, witness denied that the son of the local publican, who was a member of the committee, was the person who organised this Maypole. Mr. Pettit had experience of running dances.

Supt Somers: Is it that this four legged committee has one leg in the local public house?

Witness denied the suggestion. He agreed that there was another dance hall 200 yards away but it was on the Leinster side.

Patrick Pettit, one of the committee, stated that he was the son of Mr. Pettit, Publican. There was no truth in the accusation that he or his father intended to use this dance in connection with the licensed premises. Dances held in the other hall were considered expensive.

In reply to Supt. Somers witness said he attended with the others before Canon Hurley who told them he could not give a letter of consent and would leave the matter in the hands of the Justice.

Supt. Somers: Did Canon Hurley tell you quite clearly that he was opposed to this dance? – No.

Supt. Somers: I suggest he told you that he would not come into court and object, but was opposed to it? – No.

Sergeant McCormack, Lanesborough stated that the proposed Maypole was 60 yards and 80 yards respectively away from two local public houses. There were two other halls on the Leinster side of Lanesborough. McCrann's hall was 250 yards away from this field and the other was further on. So there was no genuine demand for further dancing facilities in Ballyleague. The site of the proposed Maypole was unsuitable for dancing.

Supt. Somers said he had one witness in Court who was objecting to the erection of this Maypole.

The Justice said that he didn't want to be considered in any sense of the word a kill-joy, but if there was one thing he was definite on it was that there was no genuine demand for a dance hall in this locality. There were two dance halls there already. The first witness didn't refer to the second dance hall at all, but it was within his (Justice's) knowledge that an application in respect of it came before him some time ago, and it was adjourned so that alterations be made and a considerable sum of money was spent on it to the satisfaction of the superintendent and the sergeant. The sergeant told him that this hall provided for the very type of people who would be going 'Maypoling'. To a question Michael Brennan said they wanted amusement for people on their side of the river.

The Justice found as a fact that there was adequate facilities for public dancing in the neighbourhood and accordingly refused the application.

Footnote: One of the conditions that Justice Kenny based his objections on was: 'No parking facilities'.

The likelihood of young people coming to a dance in 1940 by motor car was nil, and I don't think a few bikes would have caused much of a problem.

CHAPTER

29

LANESBOROUGH

Traditional Fair & Regatta

The Lanesborough Horse Fair is one of Ireland's oldest traditional fairs. Though we don't know exactly when it started, tradition has it that it was held on the 12th February each year, though in its later years the date was not so fixed.

It gradually evolved into a considerable agricultural event with the horse at its centre. Records indicate that huge numbers of people and livestock became involved and its popularity continued unabated until the advent of motorised machinery on the farm and the Tank on the battlefield. These developments reduced the reliance of the Irish horse for civil and military needs. That said, the Lanesborough Fair was still of substantial importance right up to World War II, when its significance began to wane. The business of the fair however, while greatly reduced from its 19th century prominence, continued to provide the farmers of the neighbouring districts a trading outlet.

The horse fair of Athlone was held on the last Saturday of January and it to walk to the Fair of Athlone, purchase 18 month old untrained horses, work on them intensively and have them ready for sale in Lanesborough by the 12th Feb. would not be unusual for some of our more enterprising young.

A good price for an 18 month old horse at the time of World War II would be about £45, not a bad price when a pint of Guinness would set you back 12 old pence.

Mechanically propelled vehicles were a very rare sight to see for the duration of the Second World War. Such was the heavy rationing of petrol that alternative fuels needed to be invented. The people at the Lanesborough Fair about this time were treated to visits of a lorry which ran on gas. This radical development was made possible by burning charcoal. One particular gas lorry regularly visited the fair, its owner a native of County Galway. These vehicles could be notoriously slow and not terribly practical, for example they would not be able to carry horses, but pigs were part and parcel of the Fair and such a vehicle was quite able to transport Bonhams (young pigs) from fair to fair.

The above is a postcard titled, Fair Day 1930.

Printed on the back of this postcard is the following delightful verse written by Ruth Donnellan:

Down through the years of hardship and toil,
Our ancestors sowed and they reaped from the soil,
Come 12th of February, with goods of perfection
To Lanesborough Fair they brought their collection.
The people they came in the wet and the cold,
With their birds and their animals – so I've been told
You could walk on the backs of the horses so tall,
From Lanesborough church to Ballyleague hall.

Skullduggery, Quackery and Deception

Sharp practice, wheeler dealing and sleight of hand are well known in the market place and many an unsuspecting customer has been left short changed by the application of some nefarious goings on.

As far as the horses were concerned, if a seller thought his horse was too lazy and lethargic to command a good price, then a piece of ginger inserted into an unusual orifice on the morning of the fair would give the animal a little extra *'joie de vivre'.*

On the other hand, if a horse was a little too energetic or frisky, then a live frog was inserted into the horses stomach. That usually had a calming effect on the animal.

One man, we'll call him John, was a most trustworthy type and was unaware of some of the deceitfulness and guile used by the traders, often referred to as 'Tanglers'. John came to the fair looking to sell his horse and buy a younger one.

John sold his horse to some tanglers who told him to stay where he was and they would find him a younger horse and bring it to him. Johns horse was trotted to the other end of town where a cosmetic change was brought about, his tail trimmed and mane combed, perhaps a little soot combed in, just enough to change the horses appearance, perhaps a little ginger was used to add a little friskiness? They returned the horse to John who paid them twice what he had received from them.

When John arrived back home that evening, his 'new' horse made straight for the drinking trough, it was then he realised he had his own horse back again.

Jimmy Shea of Blenavoher, (see chapter, Jimmy's Clock) Lanesborough, served as a postman for more than 40 years in the Lanesborough district. He recalled some of events associated with the annual Horse Fair.

Jimmy remembered seeing his father counting the gold sovereigns he received for his horses at the fair. The Pig Fair was held on the Friday before the Horse Fair and Jimmy recalled a very heavy snow and frost one February. The snow was so heavy on the roads that the pigs could not be walked by road so the farmers walked the pigs on the ice. One farmer would walk along the shore with a bucket of mash and the pigs would follow.

Just an example of how hard frosts could be on Fair Day in the past:

PROGRAMME (2000)

Saturday 12th Feb 2000

10.30am. All horses assemble at car park behind St Mary's Hall.

11.00am. Fair Day is officially opened by Jimmy Shea and Tim O'Shea. (Ed: Two of the parish's oldest residents.)

Parade leaves car park and travels to trading area on Dublin Road/Upper Main St.

12.30pm. Co-op Share Launch: Official launch and opening of share offer for the Lough Ree Development Co-op. Special guest: Lanesborough native Dessie Hynes. Venue: The Green opposite St Mary's Church.

1.30pm. Fair Day Drama:

A special variety show with recitations by Tommie Murray, Jim Nolan (Carlow) and Vincent Pierce (Roscommon). Music and Dance. Show repeated 3.00pm. Venue. Marquee on The Green.

2.00pm. Horse Pulling and Donkey Derby.

New features for the Fair Day. Venue: Tommy Kearns field (GAA pitch adjacent to Mushroom Tunnels, Longford Road).

3.00pm. Champion Horse and Pony. Adjudication for these special prizes will begin. Judges include International Show Jumper Capt. Gerard Flynn. Venue: Tommy Kearns field.

3.00pm. Fair Day Drama – Second performance. Marquee on The Green.

4.00pm. Millennium Pony Auction – One of the highlights of the day. Auction of Pony will take place at Lanesborough Branch Library.

4.30pm. Fair Day 'Tug-O-War' – A new feature as teams from public house east and west of the Shannon compete in a major battle of strength and wills. Venue: Paddy Greens field, adjacent to Lifebelt Bar and Lounge, Ballyleague.

10.00pm. The Fair Dance. Dancing to 'Rig the Jig'. Drama performance – 'The Mummers'* by Sancho Galileo, performed by the Lanesborough and Ballyleague Players, directed by Gus Hanley and Loretta Gallagher. Venue: Lough Ree Arms. Come early to avoid disappointment...

**Mummers or mumming is a tradition of re-telling old stories and fables, while dressed in various masks. Some of these masks can be grotesque, others perhaps birds and others variations of the human face.*

Sunday 13th Feb 2000

1.30pm. Vintage Cars and Tractors – Assemble at Longford County Council car park – behind St Mary's Hall Lanesborough.
1.30pm. Fair Weekend Dog Show Entries taken for ten classes at The Green opposite St Mary's Church.
2.00pm. Vintage Parade – Cars, Tractors and other machinery leaves car park and travels to St Mary's Church. Display will continue until 5.00pm. (Road closed between Church and Swan Tavern)
2.15pm. Dog Show Opens. 10 Prizes.
4.00pm. Presentation of prizes to Dog Owners and vintage car and tractor owners.
5.00pm. **End of vintage display.**

REGATTA 2000

It seems the millennium was a good time for reviving old traditions, as well as the Horse Fair, the year 2000 also saw the return of the Lanesborough Regatta. Organised under the auspices of the Lough Ree Area Development Co-Operative.

In the programme produced to mark the occasion, Mairéad O'Shea wrote **'The Story of the Regatta'**:

It's over forty years since the Black Island Oarsmen made their way through the waters of the river Shannon to take part in the Lanesborough Regatta and now for the first time in decades an age old tradition has finally been revived.

The Lanesborough Regatta was an annual event that drew crowds from all around Co. Longford and beyond, with oarsmen from the Black Islands and Saints Island taking part in the sporting activities. The last regatta is believed to have taken place in 1952 when a series of boating races and novelty events were enjoyed by locals and visitors alike.

The Regatta of Lanesborough/Ballyleague was one of Ireland's best known traditional water sports events throughout the 1930s, '40s, '50s and '60s. In 1929 rowers from all over the country competed in the first recorded regatta and now, some 40 plus years after the last event the tradition is to be revived.

A group of locals joined together in association with the Lough Ree Sub Aqua Club and the Lough Ree Development organisation got together to form an organising committee, dedicated to the revival of the traditional regatta.

The Lanesborough Regatta was officially launched on Sunday last and the large crowd in attendance proved the local level of interest and enthusiasm. Mr. Joe Pyke of the Irish Amateur Rowing Union officially launched the regatta.

This years revived Lanesborough Regatta will take place on Sunday 27th August and great plans are underway to make it a terrific family day out.

This year rowing clubs from Limerick, Galway, Fermanagh, Offaly, Leitrim and Dublin will take part in the revival of the river Shannon Regatta. Past cups and trophies have been uncovered for the revived event and John Casey of Lanesborough was kind enough to supply an old programme of the 1931 event and an old photo of the 1952 ladies Carrick-On-Shannon team.

The Carrick-on-Shannon Ladies Rowing Eight 1964.

Michael Sorahan PRO of the committee says the idea was born in conjunction with the revival of the old Lanesborough horse fair as an effort to reintroduce some of the old traditional cultural events. There is no rowing club in Lanesborough despite the fact that the River Shannon has always been the focal point of development in the area and this was another major factor in the decision to revive the regatta. As Michael said: "Athlone, Carrick-On-Shannon and Tullamore all have rowing clubs and we hope the revival of the regatta will develop some interest in a Lanesborough rowing club."

The regatta involves a variety of boating competitions such as, Single and Double Scull, Motor Boat Races and Yacht Races to name but a few. It's not all about boating however, as traditionally the regatta has always been a family day out with a series of fun activities for everyone. At this years revived event regatta goers can look forward to a canoeing race, a pleasure boat race, a raft race and a series of swimming events. music and entertainment will also be provided with a BBQ and bouncing castle for children.

Enda Oates, well known actor of Glenroe, Upwardly Mobile and Fair City, and also a native Roscommon man, will present at the first race of the Regatta. Enda will make a little bit of history as his own father PJ Oates was a renowned oarsman and won many competitions in previous regattas.

One man who attended many previous regattas and recalls many memories is Jimmy Shea of Blenahover. Indeed Jimmy and his cousin Tim Shea recently opened the revived Lanesborough horse fair. Jimmy remembers the regatta as a great day out with people coming from all over Longford and Roscommon to enjoy the days festivities. Indeed, he recalls the day PJ Oates called at his home to borrow a boat for the regatta. "I remember the day PJ called for the boat and sure he went on to win the competition that day."

Jimmy also remembers the various competitions that took place at the Regatta including the duck race and the greasy pole.

The greasy pole competition involved a number of swimmers travelling out to a pole in the water from which they had to remove a particular object. The only problem being that the pole was covered in grease and proved extremely difficult to manoeuvre. Mary

McGushin is another local who recalls the numerous competitions she attended as a young teenager such as the duck race and the greasy pole, with one poor unfortunate man losing his false teeth doubled over in laughter. There were also tug-o-war competitions, musical entertainment and dancing.

If this years revived regatta is as much fun as those of yesteryear, then August 27th is a date for your diary.

In the same programmes produced for the 2000 Regatta, Pat Leavy contributed the following piece:

We are reminded that it was a very famous event that started in the early 1930s and continued successfully until the late fifties. It was revived in the early sixties but never attracted the same level of interest as before and eventually faded out completely.

The old Regatta we are told was a major sporting and social occasion, probably responsible for the largest gathering of people to the town and bridge area in the whole year, as it was held in mid-summer.

The major events were boating races for men which consisted of single and double sculls, with a race or two over a shorter course.

The main event carried a prize of £3.00s which was regarded as well worth fighting for. (Amazingly, £3.00 in the 1930s would be worth £245 today – 2024)

By present day procedures the boat racing of yesteryear was to say the least, quite different, Lanes did not exist, competitors usually four or five per race would line up facing the lake.

The procedure for starting was that either Michael Ryan or Jack Farrell of Ballyleague would discharge a round from their shot-gun, then it was 'helter skelter' to round the barrel marker placed some few hundred yards from the cut.

First round the barrel had a major advantage, as crashing was the order of the day, with loss of ground and in many cases loss of temper!

Those who took part were some from the local area, Ballyleague and Lanesborough, but the majority were natives of the Shannon Shore on both sides.

On the West, Roscommon side, they came from Gardenstown, Portnahinch and Knockcroghery and on the Longford side, from

Rathcline, Cashel, Saints Island and Glasson. Some of the great oarsmen originated in the islands and their boats and the rowing technique was second to none. Lest the reader would assume there was little to the regatta except serious competition there was also a much lighter side to the day.

I refer of course to events such as the Duck Race and the Greasy Pole, the latter being a real fun event.

A long pole, coated with grease was suspended over the water's edge, with a flag placed at its end.

The task was simple, competitors would be obliged to retrieve the flag, and it is recalled with great hilarity that a local man, Mick Duignan, tried to negotiate the pole without bothering to tog-out, he didn't even bother to remove his hat. It was said he received a small bit of encouragement from a bottle and a large cheer from the crowd, the outcome was inevitable, he bit the dust, or at least made a bit of a splash.

In later years Ned Connaughton from Moneen emerged as the hero of this event and would finish the evening with displays of diving from the top of the bridge, with spectators three to four deep to observe this daring feat.

The Duck Race was also a popular event, with a duck having its wings clipped, would be pursued by the best swimmers. The Duck, because of its ability to dive and its streamlined features generally had the last 'quack'.

J. Oates remembered that one of the best boats he ever saw was the property of the late Michael Farrell, Shannon View, and was always in popular demand. Michael Farrell was always to the fore in his support and encouragement of sporting events. His boat would receive a full overhaul, and be painted by local tradesman Joe Diffley, who had a workshop but a stones throw from Shannon View.

Public Houses – Harold and Pettits on the Ballyleague side and Ger Farrells and Thomas Casey's did a roaring trade, and the Regatta Dance in McCrann's Hall finished up the social side of the day.

Swimming Gala – Ger Farrell holding towel.

Wouldn't it be great if at some future date the Regatta could be re-revived. (Ed)

CHAPTER

30

LIKE A SCENE FROM THE WILD WEST

Lanesborough P.O. Dynamited!

At almost exactly the same time as Butch Cassidy and the Sundance Kid were blowing up banks and trains in the U.S.A., an audacious attempt to do the same was made on our own Post Office here in Lanesborough.

(The exact source of the following article is unknown but the Longford Leader *would be a good guess)*

LANESBORO

THE POST OFFICE BLOWN UP MIRACULOUS ESCAPE OF THE INMATES FULL DETAILS (1897).

At about 10.30 on Friday morning last, intelligence reached Longford that at about 4.00am on the same morning an attempt had been made to blow up the Post Office in Lanesboro' with dynamite. At first no one believed the story. The very notion that a dynamite bomb would find its way to Lanesboro' to be used for the destruction of two of the most inoffensive creatures on the face of the earth was, to put it mildly, scouted. *(To mock, ridicule and treat with disdain, Olde English – Ed.)*

However, later intelligence confirmed the news and left no doubt that one of the most diabolical and unheard of crimes in this part of the country had been attempted.

It appears that on the preceding night, the inmates of the Post Office, Mr. Dunne, the servant girl and the mistress of the establishment, an old and most respected lady, Miss Costello, retired to rest in the ordinary way. At about 4.00am they were aroused from their slumbers by a most terrific explosion, and the crash of breaking glass on all sides. So loud was the report that it immediately awakened all the people in the village of Lanesboro', many of whom thought 'judgement day' had come and hurriedly dressed and ran out into the street. The police, too, were early on the scene. Vast clouds of dust were about the Post Office and to there, all made their way. A terrible sight met their eyes.

Every pane of glass in the windows of the Post Office, as well as in the neighbouring houses were discovered to be smashed into smithereens.

It was at once apparent that some person had deliberately placed some explosive on the sill of the Post Office window and this explosion had wrought dreadful havoc and nearly made the place a scene of frightful carnage and destruction. The window sill was clean cut in two and this was evidence that some considerable time had been occupied in making the arrangements for the explosion. It is pretty well known that dynamite has an upward tendency when exploding unless a heavy weight is placed on it.

This window looks into a room which is used partly as a sitting room and partly as a post office. The latter is railed off from the former by a curtain. From the way in which the explosion took place, it is pretty clear that the miscreant had a twofold object in view. One was to destroy the official documents of the Post Office, the other was to kill or frighten to death the poor old lady of the Post Office. That both were fairly 'oiled' is a subject for congratulation, not, however, to be attributed to the ruffian who placed the bomb there, but to his ignorance of the way to use his deadly weapon.

(I can find no definition for 'oiled' other than lubed up or drunk? (Ed)

When the people rushed down, they were much relieved and cheered to see Mr. Dunne, Miss Costello and the servant girl come out of the ruins in safety. Hard and deep maledictions were placed on the head of the would be murderer of innocent people. When things had somewhat settled down and an examination of the place could be made, it was found the following damage had been done. The furniture of the sitting room was smashed. The window and frame were broken to splinters, all the windows in the house and the house opposite were broken, and the ceiling of the courthouse was thrown down by the force of the concussion.

The place was at once practically taken possession of by the police, who headed by County Inspector McDermott and District Inspector McCaffrey of Ballymahon, have been since doing all they can to unravel the mystery. It is not likely however that they will succeed. Various and startling theories are on foot regarding the authors of the outrage. It may be unravelled, but we do not think it will.

Colonel Majendie, the Inspector of Explosives, has arrived on the scene to hold his enquiry. The result will be purely speculative however, unless some clue turns up other than any the police have yet got.

CHAPTER

31

A MYSTERY

Can anybody help?

In all my collections and paraphernalia regarding Lanesborough/ Ballyleague, the below transcript of a memorial stone that was in the graveyard at Moydow, is the only reference I have ever come across that suggests Lanesborough was once known as Brackaugh.

The Ordnance Survey of the 1830s fixed the boundaries of Townlands. It is clear from the pre-plantation maps that exist that many smaller named areas were subsumed in the new townland structure. As a fixed townland name gained in prominence the other names tended to fade out unless they were preserved in the folk memory.

The name O'Farrell has of course a very strong local connection but has anybody else heard of Brackaugh?

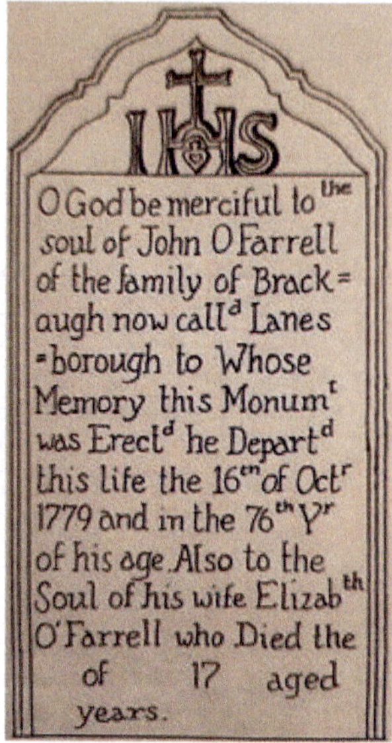
IHS

O God be merciful to the
soul of John O Farrell
of the family of Brack=
augh now call^d Lanes
=borough to Whose
Memory this Monum^t
was Erect^d he Depart^d
this life the 16th of Oct^r
1779 and in the 76th Y^r
of his age. Also to the
Soul of his wife Elizab^th
O'Farrell who Died the
of 17 aged
years.

MAPS, LETTERS AND PHOTOGRAPHS

CHAPTER

32

Many of the letters and photographs in John Casey's collection have been included in the relative chapters where appropriate. The following are some interesting letters and photographs that don't directly relate.

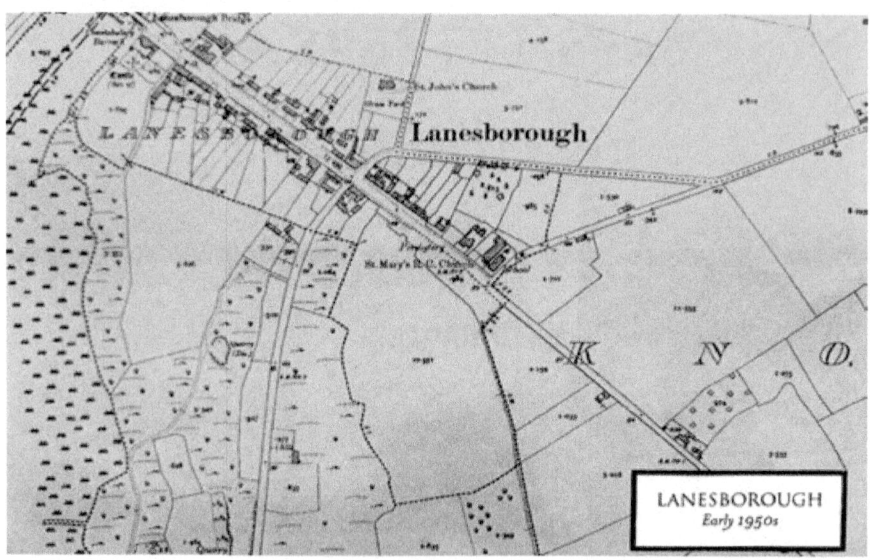

LANESBOROUGH
Early 1950s

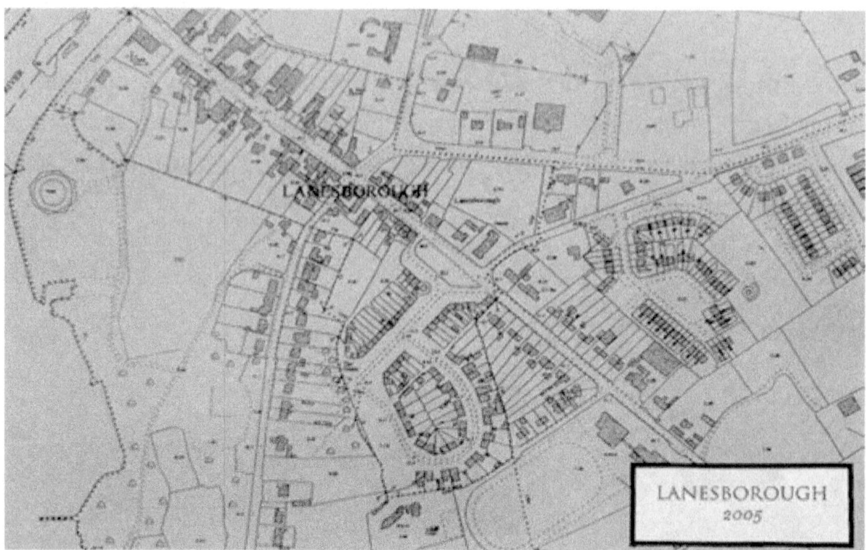
LANESBOROUGH
2005

Two maps showing how the town developed with the opening of the bog:

PROVIDENCE
May 2. 1895

Dear Peter
I wish to inform you I have got here on this day I sailed on the Thursday after leaving home. I got on well so far as travelling goes but everything was very dear my passage from Queenstown was £4.00 and 16s from Roscommon to Queenstown we had a very nice passage only Saturday night and that blew a strong storm but the boat was good and we were not afraid her name is the Teutonic. I made my way first class as regard this we were put on an Island called Ellis Island and had to pass a strict examination as to Doctors and where you were going and so forth and I got off on the first boat from the Island and was in time to catch the 5oclock boat for Providence and travelled all night I cant say how I will get on in the future but I was lucky up to this there is a very bad account in that City at present but I am only after arriving and I wont say any thing until I see further I will write when I get a job if not I will try some where else I hope yourself and Maggie is well and all the family and also my own poor children as for the rest of the family I am not put about do all you can to make them put down the crop I met with John Cox since I came but he was working I can travel well in a strange country so long as I have money and I get respect everywhere since I left home but I could get none at home. I will write soon again.
I remain yours truly.

The living relatives of the author of this letter wish to remain anonymous.

Morrisons Hotel.
Dawson Street.
Dublin
August 22nd 1891

My dear Sir.

In anticipation of the change of policy by the proposed new Directorate of the "Freeman's Journal". I have been requested by a large and influential body of our friends to start a first class morning and evening newspaper to advocate the principals of home rule for Ireland and Independent Action in the House of Commons. At a preliminary meeting it was decided before issuing a prospectus, to secure guarantees for not less than ten thousand pounds. I am happy to tell you two thirds of that sum has been promptly signed for As there is no time to be lost in carrying out the proposed untaking. I now enclose your forms which kindly fill up yourself and ask your friends to do likewise, returning them to me at above address at your early convenience. The shares will be one pound each.

I remain your faithful servant.
Charles Steward Parnell

This letter from Charles Stewart Parnell was written to Mr Bernard McKenna who was the secretary of the Rathcline Branch of the Irish Land League Party.

Bernard McKenna was the Principle of Tullyvrane School at the time of this letter. It has always been a local rumour that Charles Stewart Parnell actually stayed in Tullyvrane schoolhouse overnight. It is alleged that Mr Parnell left his slippers behind ...

SARAH KILLIAN'S SCHOOL ESSAY, 1892

Moher,
Lanesborough,

20th January 1892.

To: Miss Annie Hanly,
Clooneigh,
Roscommon.

Dear Annie,

A very large meeting was held in Ballyleague on the 17th January to uphold the principles of our late Chief C.S. Parnell. A vast crowd of people attended which was composed principally of old and young men from the following parishes: Cloontuskert, Kilgefin, Curraghroe, Kilglass, Strokestown, Kiltruscan, Kilbride, Knockcroghery, Roscommon, etc., all with their bands and banners and musical instruments, and played marches and airs suitable to the occasion. These men came form a distance varying from six to eight and twelve miles.

Great preparations were made for the reception of the members of parliament, viz. the houses were decorated with laurels and a great part of the band-men wore green in their hats, etc. The members of parliament arrived about half past two in a car or brake, together with many other local men. The thousands of people who were awaiting the arrival of the members marched on with their bands and banners to welcome them. About three o'clock the members took their places on the platform, where speeches were delivered by them and other leading local men. The speeches were received with great applause by all present, which lasted for over three hours, and was terminated by the members being entertained, after which all returned to their homes, much pleased with the day's success.

I am, Dear Annie,

Yours very sincerely,

Sarah Killian.

Sarah Killian would be distant relative of John Killian of Fermoyle. Here she writes to a school friend about a meeting in Ballyleague that is self explanatory.

Alfred McCrann and his brother Paddy in an early automobile approximately at the turn of the 20th century.

Two pictures of a pony and cart advertising Lyons Tea pre-war. We have no information as to exactly when these were taken.

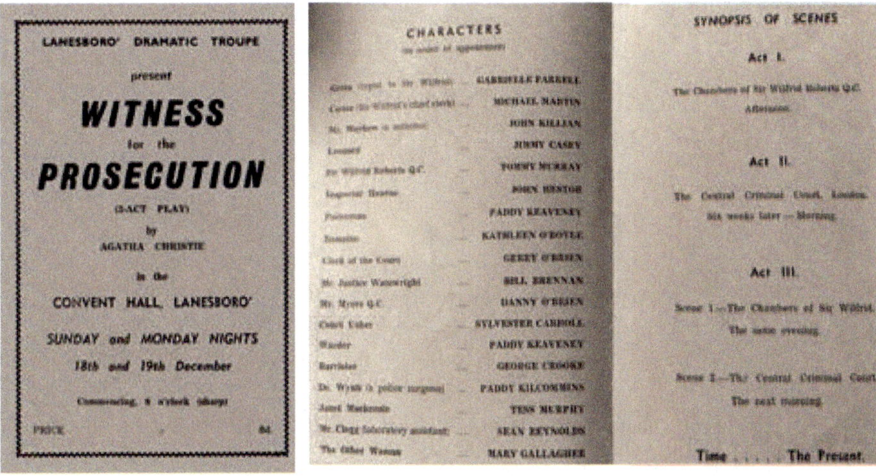

LANESBORO' DRAMATIC TROUPE
present
WITNESS
for the
PROSECUTION
(3-ACT PLAY)
by
AGATHA CHRISTIE
in the
CONVENT HALL, LANESBORO'
SUNDAY and MONDAY NIGHTS
18th and 19th December
Commencing, 8 o'clock (sharp)
PRICE ... 6d.

CHARACTERS

MICHAEL MARTIN
JOHN KILLIAN
JIMMY CASEY
TOMMY MURRAY
PADDY KEAVENEY
KATHLEEN O'BOYLE
BILL BRENNAN
DANNY O'BRIEN
SYLVESTER CARROLL
PADDY KEAVENEY
GEORGE CROOKE
PADDY KILCOMMINS
TESS MURPHY
SEAN REYNOLDS
MARY GALLAGHER

SYNOPSIS OF SCENES

Act I.
The Chambers of Sir Wilfrid Robarts Q.C.
Afternoon.

Act II.
The Central Criminal Court, London.
Six weeks later — Morning.

Act III.
Scene 1 — The Chambers of Sir Wilfrid.
The same evening.
Scene 2 — The Central Criminal Court.
The next morning.

Time . . . . . The Present.

The cover and inside of the Programme for the production in 1960 of the Agatha Christie play: 'WITNESS FOR THE PROSECUTION'.

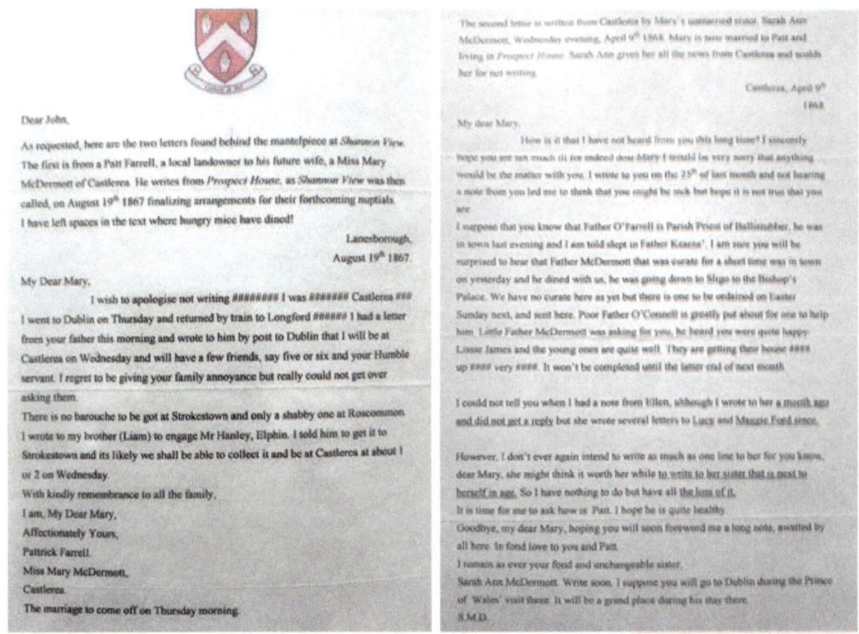

Dear John,

As requested, here are the two letters found behind the mantelpiece at *Shannon View*. The first is from a Patt Farrell, a local landowner to his future wife, a Miss Mary McDermott of Castlerea. He writes from *Prospect House*, as *Shannon View* was then called, on August 19th 1867 finalizing arrangements for their forthcoming nuptials. I have left spaces in the text where hungry mice have dined!

Lanesborough,
August 19th 1867.

My Dear Mary,

I wish to apologise not writing ######## I was ####### Castlerea ### I went to Dublin on Thursday and returned by train to Longford ###### I had a letter from your father this morning and wrote to him by post to Dublin that I will be at Castlerea on Wednesday and will have a few friends, say five or six and your Humble servant. I regret to be giving your family annoyance but really could not get over asking them.

There is no barouche to be got at Strokestown and only a shabby one at Roscommon. I wrote to my brother (Liam) to engage Mr Hanley, Elphin. I told him to get it to Strokestown and its likely we shall be able to collect it and be at Castlerea at about 1 or 2 on Wednesday.

With kindly remembrance to all the family,
I am, My Dear Mary,
Affectionately Yours,
Patrick Farrell.
Miss Mary McDermott,
Castlerea.
The marriage to come off on Thursday morning.

The second letter is written from Castlerea by Mary's unmarried sister, Sarah Ann McDermott, Wednesday evening, April 9th 1868. Mary is now married to Patt and living in *Prospect House*. Sarah Ann gives her all the news from Castlerea and scolds her for not writing.

Castlerea, April 9th
1868

My dear Mary,

How is it that I have not heard from you this long time? I sincerely hope you are not much ill for indeed dear Mary I would be very sorry that anything would be the matter with you. I wrote to you on the 25th of last month and not hearing a note from you led me to think that you might be sick but hope it is not true that you are.

I suppose that you know that Father O'Farrell is Parish Priest of Ballintubber, he was in town last evening and I am told slept in Father Kearns'. I am sure you will be surprised to hear that Father McDermott that was curate for a short time was in town on yesterday and he dined with us, he was going down to Sligo to the Bishop's Palace. We have no curate here as yet but there is one to be ordained on Easter Sunday next, and sent here. Poor Father O'Connell is greatly put about for one to help him. Little Father McDermott was asking for you, he heard you were quite happy. Lissie James and the young ones are quite well. They are getting their house #### up #### very ####. It won't be completed until the latter end of next month.

I could not tell you when I had a note from Ellen, although I wrote to her a month ago and did not get a reply but she wrote several letters to Lucy and Maggie Ford since.

However, I don't ever again intend to write as much as one line to her for you know, dear Mary, she might think it worth her while to write to her sister that is next to herself in age. So I have nothing to do but have all the loss of it.

It is time for me to ask how is Patt. I hope he is quite healthy.

Goodbye, my dear Mary, hoping you will soon forward me a long note, awaited by all here. In fond love to you and Patt.

I remain as ever your fond and unchangeable sister,
Sarah Ann McDermott. Write soon. I suppose you will go to Dublin during the Prince of Wales' visit there. It will be a grand place during his stay there.
S.M.D.

Two letters of 1867. These letters were found during a renovation of Shannon View and passed to John for safe keeping.

Commonwealth of Massachusetts

Town of Lanesborough

Newton Memorial Town Hall
Post Office Box 1492
Lanesborough, MA 01237
Tel. (413) 442-1167
FAX 443-5811

OFFICE OF THE
BOARD OF SELECTMEN

November 13, 2007

Dear Friends Across the Sea,

What a wonderful time we all had with you when you visited us last month. We wish we could have had more time together to learn more about each other and to share more of our town, its people and its history.

We especially wish to thank you for the gifts you brought us. The painting is hanging above the fireplace in the Selectmen's office, much to the dismay of the library people! And the map is a great addition to our collection of historical pictures of our town and yours.

We do hope this exchange will continue, especially between our children through their schools. What a wonderful opportunity to learn more about each other and our countries.

Until we meet again,

William Prendergast Jr.

John Goerlach

Gae Elfenbein

The Town of Lanesborough is an equal opportunity provider. Discrimination is prohibited by Federal Law.

A thank you letter from Lanesborough, Massachusetts following a visit from our own community in 2007.

The following three items were given to John Casey by Louis Rhattigans' wife over 20 years ago. All are of a great age.

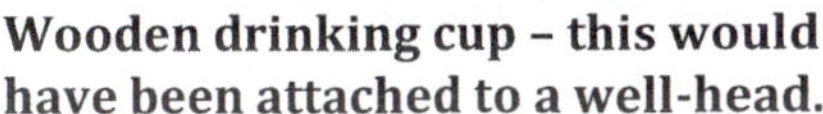
Wooden drinking cup – this would have been attached to a well-head.

A candle stick or rush holder.

Finally, two pictures of a copper gunpowder flask that belonged to Andrew Rhattigan. Andrew was a member of the local Lanesborough militia circa 1790 –1810. The second photograph shows clearly where Andrew has scratched his initials on the flask.

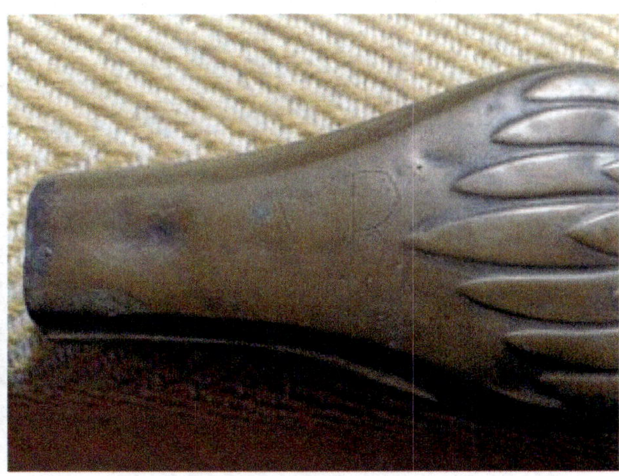

Mentioned in the Chapter: Tributes, Seán Cahill – is a picture of the 1969 Passion Play and the cast of the 1936 version.

Tommy Murray has provided a number of other photographs which will be of interest to many.

Another photograph of the earlier 1936 Passion Play, with L-R: Tom Gilloolly, Ned Dempsey, unsure, Mary Murray, kneeling in front of the cross: Anne Glennon, unsure, Mike Martin, Tom Hynes and Charlie Rhattigan.

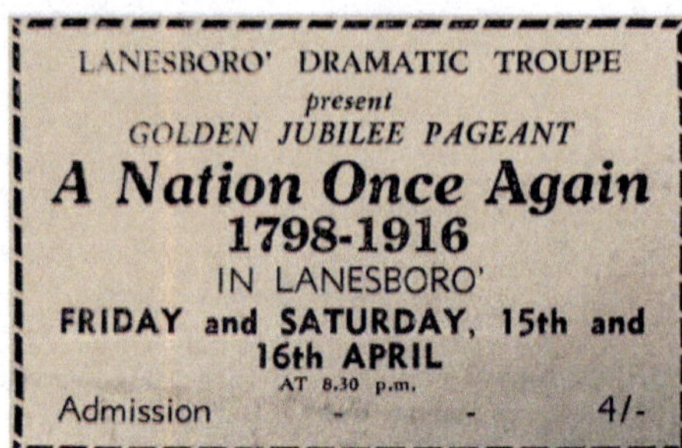

LANESBORO' DRAMATIC TROUPE
present
GOLDEN JUBILEE PAGEANT
A Nation Once Again
1798-1916
IN LANESBORO'
FRIDAY and SATURDAY, 15th and 16th APRIL
AT 8.30 p.m.
Admission - - 4/-

An advert for the production of 'A Nation Once Again' which was produced on the 50th anniversary of the Easter Rising.

A re-enactment of a scene from the GPO.

The Orchestra used for the production of 'A Nation Once Again'. Pictured L-R: Jim Donlan, Mike Shields, Patsy Fayne, Sister Immaculata, John Donlans' daughter Elizabeth?, Sister Gerard, Joe Gallagher and Dan Kelly.

The organising committee for the 1966 production.
Back row L-R: Joe Gallagher, Jimmy Casey, Seán Cahill, John Hestor and Eddie Murray.
Front: Danny O'Brien, Father Chris Lynch and Tommy Murray.

PICTURES FROM THE PAGEANT

At Grave of O'Donovan Rossa: John Hester, Tom McGrath, Paddy Kilcommins, Tommy Murray, Pat Keaveney, Tom Maxwell – (others hidden).

Leaders in meeting with Owen McNiall (from left): Tommy Murray, Paddy Kilcommins, Luke Farrell, Tom McGrath, John Hester, Noel Gallagher, Eddie Murray and Jimmy Casey (hidden).

Pearse reads the Proclamation at GPO. Sylvester Carroll, John Hester, Paddy Kilcommins, Tommy Murray, Tom McGrath, Jack Murray, George Crookes, Harry Hennessy and Seán Reynolds.

A rehearsal for the pageant – at the head on the Pipes is Tony Murphy, father of the late Stella O'Sullivan.

Pupils of N.S. 1948.

Pupils of N.S. 1949.

Cast of OLD KING COLE Pantomime 1967.

Cast of DICKWHITTINGTO N Pantomime 1968.

Chorus of DICKWHITTINGTO N Pantomime 1968.

ACKNOWLEDGMENTS

CHAPTER 1	**Troubled Times** Longford's Republican Story 1900 -2000 - Seán Ó Súilleabháin The *Longford Leader* John Casey Archive, Tommy Murray
CHAPTER 2	**Lanesborough Memories** *by: John Casey*
CHAPTER 3	**Memories of my Father's Forge** *by: Tommy Murray*
CHAPTER 4	**Pat Fee** John Casey Archive
CHAPTER 5	**Jimmy Murray** John Casey Archive
CHAPTER 6	**Fr. Joseph Murphy** Fr. Joseph Murphy S.J. - A Journey *by: John Casey*
CHAPTER 7	**The Doctor** Joan McMahon (*Née* Rhattigan) (written 2005) The *Longford Leader* Census of Ireland 1911. John Casey Archive
CHAPTER 8	**The Davys Family** Notes taken from the Davys Family Records, arranged for publication by: S.F. O'Cianain M.B. printed in the *Longford Leader* Oct 10th, 17th, 24th & 31st & Nov 7th 1931
CHAPTER 9	**Two who Travelled** John Casey Archive The Leavy Family
CHAPTER 10	**Michael Casey, Craftsman** Kevin Casey Double - Vision Michael Casey Exhibition Catalogue The *Irish Times* John Casey, Family Archive
CHAPTER 11	**Jimmy's Clock** *by: Mairéad O'Shea*
CHAPTER 12	**Tributes** John Casey, Tommy Murray
CHAPTER 13	**I Have Often Walked Down This Street Before** John Casey, Christine McDonagh, Michael Connaughton
CHAPTER 14	**The Hunt for Lincoln's Killer** The Irish in the American Civil WAR - Damian Shie
CHAPTER 15	**Mills** County Longford Historical Society and Rathcline 'PATHWAYS TO THE PAST', both by Tommy Murray, John Casey Archive

CHAPTER 16 **Rathcline Castle**
County Longford Historical Society
London gazette 1861. John Casey, Archive

CHAPTER 17 **The Bridge**
Canon Hurley's notes
Rathcline, 'PATHWAYS TO THE PAST',
Chapter *'Crossing The Water'* by: John Casey
Circa 1830 Survey of Roscommon

CHAPTER 18 **St. Mary's and St. John's**
John Casey Archive CONSTITUTIONS AND CANONS ECCLESIASTICAL 1840

CHAPTER 19 **A Firm Foundation**
John Casey Archive

CHAPTER 20 **Tales of Curreen**
John Casey Archive

CHAPTER 21 **The School in the Field**
by: John Casey

CHAPTER 22 **Inchcleuran in Lough Ree**
by: Seán Cahill

CHAPTER 23 **The Rathcline Man-Trap**
John Casey Archive Athlone Castle Museum

CHAPTER 24 **Eviction Stone (1814)**
by: John Casey

CHAPTER 25 **Important Visitors to Lanesborough**
Irish Times 22/08/1885 Reported evidence of Constable J McCoy The *Irish Times*
John Casey Archive

CHAPTER 26 **Edwardian Matchmaking**
John Casey Archive

CHAPTER 27 **Newtowncashel - Population Exodus**
John Casey Archive

CHAPTER 28 **Lanesborough / Ballyleague Divided - a Local Disagreement** *Longford Leader*

CHAPTER 29 **Lanesborough Traditional Fair and Regatta**
Regatta Programme 2000 Mairead O'Shea, Pat Leavy,
John Casey Archive

CHAPTER 30 **Like a Scene from the Wild West**
Longford Leader

CHAPTER 31 **A Mystery**
John Casey Archive

CHAPTER 32 **Maps, Letters and Photographs**
John Casey Archive, Tommy Murray

Printed in Great Britain
by Amazon

46617084R00116